I0013227

There is a reason the U.S. Air Force has one of the best cyberwarfare weapon system programs. This book pulls together 4 key Air Force publications on the Air Force Intranet Network Control (AFINC).

| AFI 17-2AFINC, VOL. 1 | AIR FORCE INTRANET NETWORK CONTROL (AFINC) TRAINING | 23 May 2017 |
|---|---|---|
| AFI 17-2AFINC, VOL. 2 | AIR FORCE INTRANET NETWORK CONTROL (AFINC) STANDARDIZATION AND EVALUATION PROGRAM | 23 May 2017 |
| AFI 17-2AFINC, VOL. 3 | AIR FORCE INTRANET NETWORK CONTROL (AFINC) OPERATIONS AND PROCEDURES | 23 May 2017 |
| AFI33-115 | AIR FORCE INFORMATION TECHNOLOGY (IT) SERVICE MANAGEMENT | 16 Sep 2014 |

AFI 17-2AFINC prescribes basic policy and guidance for training United States Air Force Intranet Network Control (AFINC) crewmembers. Mission readiness and effective employment are achieved through the development and mastery of core competencies for AFINC crewmembers. It provides cyberspace operations examiners and cybercrew members with procedures and evaluation criteria used during performance evaluations on the Air Force Intranet Control weapon system. This AFI provides specific information and grading criteria for each crew position, special mission qualification (SMQ), instructor upgrade qualification, and Stan/Eval examiner objectivity evaluations. All evaluations fall under the Qualification (QUAL), Mission (MSN) or Spot (SPOT) categories. It prescribes procedures for operating the AFINC weapon system by providing mission planning guidelines, standard operating procedures, minimum forces, terrain, communication plan, vulnerability/operating window, deconfliction plan, abort criteria and contingency plan and weapon system health/status.

If your organization is not using this information as a general guide for developing your own tactics and procedures, then you are at a severe disadvantage. Air Force has been doing this for a while and they provide defensive and operational guidance that can be followed universally to protect critical computer networks.

**Why buy a book you can download for free? We print this so you don't have to.**

When a new standard is released, an engineer prints it out, punches holes and puts it in a 3-ring binder. While this is not a big deal for a 5 or 10-page document, many cyber documents are over 100 pages and printing a large document is a time-consuming effort. So, an engineer that's paid $75 an hour is spending hours simply printing out the tools needed to do the job. That's time that could be better spent doing engineering. We publish these documents so engineers can focus on what they were hired to do – engineering.

A list of **Cybersecurity Standards** we publish is attached at the end of this document.

Other titles published by 4<sup>th</sup> Watch Publishing Co.

*BY ORDER OF THE SECRETARY*
*OF THE AIR FORCE*

*AIR FORCE INSTRUCTION 17-2AFINC*
*VOLUME 1*

*23 MAY 2017*

*Cyberspace*

*AIR FORCE INTRANET NETWORK*
*CONTROL (AFINC) TRAINING*

## COMPLIANCE WITH THIS PUBLICATION IS MANDATORY

**ACCESSIBILITY:** Publications and forms are available for downloading or ordering on the e- Publishing website at www.e-Publishing.af.mil

**RELEASABILITY:** There are no releaseability restrictions on this publication

OPR: AF/A3CX/A6CX

Certified by: AF/A3C/A6C
(Col Donald J. Fielden)
Pages: 40

This instruction implements Air Force (AF) Policy Directive (AFPD) 17-2, *Cyberspace Operations* and references AF Instruction (AFI) 17-202, Volume 1, *Cybercrew Training*. It establishes the minimum AF standards for training and qualifying/certifying personnel for performing crewmember duties on the Air Force Intranet Control (AFINC) weapon system. This publication applies to all military and civilian AF personnel, members of the AF Reserve Command (AFRC), Air National Guard (ANG), third-party governmental employee and contractor support personnel in accordance with appropriate provisions contained in memoranda support agreements and AF contracts.

The authorities to waive wing/unit level requirements in this publication are identified with a Tier ("T-0, T-1, T-2, T-3") number following the compliance statement. See AFI 33-360, *Publications and Forms Management*, Table 1.1 for a description of the authorities associated with the Tier numbers. Submit requests for waivers through the chain of command to the appropriate Tier waiver approval authority, or alternately, to the Publication OPR for non-tiered compliance items. This instruction requires collecting and maintaining information protected by the Privacy Act of 1974 (5 U.S.C. 552a). System of Records Notices F036 AF PC C, Military Personnel Records System, and OPM/GOVT-1, General Personnel Records, apply. Units may supplement this instruction. All supplements will be coordinated through HQ AFSPC/A2/3/6T prior to publication. Process supplements as shown in AFI 33-360. Major Command (MAJCOM) supplements will be coordinated with USAF A3C/A6C. Guidance provided by the lead major command will contain specific training requirements unique to individual and crew positions. Send recommended changes or comments to HQ USAF/A3C/A6C, 1480 Air Force Pentagon,

Washington, DC 20330-1480, through appropriate channels, using AF Form 847, *Recommendation for Change of Publication*. When collecting and maintaining information protect it by the Privacy Act of 1974 authorized by 10 U.S.C. 8013. Ensure that all records created as a result of processes prescribed in this publication are maintained in accordance with AF Manual (AFMAN) 33-363, *Management of Records*, and disposed of in accordance with the AF Records Disposition Schedule (RDS).

**Chapter 1— GENERAL INFORMATION**                                                                          **5**

    1.1.    Training Objectives....................................................................................... 5

    1.2.    Abbreviations,.............................................................................................. 5

    1.3.    Responsibilities:.......................................................................................... 5

    1.4.    Training....................................................................................................... 7

    1.5.    Training Concepts and Policies: ................................................................. 8

    1.6.    Experienced Crewmember Requirements.................................................... 9

Table    1.1.    Experienced Crewmember Requirements (T-3)............................................ 10

    1.7.    RCP Policy and Management:....................................................................... 10

    1.8.    Training Mission Program Development: .................................................... 11

    1.9.    Training Records and Reports: ..................................................................... 11

    1.10.    Crewmember Utilization Policy: .................................................................. 12

    1.11.    Sortie Allocation and Unit Manpower Guidance:........................................ 12

    1.12.    Training on Operational Missions. ............................................................... 12

    1.13.    In-Unit Training Time Limitations:.............................................................. 12

Table    1.2.    In-Unit Training Time Limitations Active Duty (Calendar Days). (T-3)............... 13

    1.14.    Periodic and End-of-Cycle Training Reports. ............................................. 13

    1.15.    Waiver Authority: ........................................................................................ 13

**Chapter 2— INITIAL QUALIFICATION TRAINING**                                                       **15**

    2.1.    General......................................................................................................... 15

    2.2.    Formal Training............................................................................................ 15

    2.3.    Local Training.............................................................................................. 15

    2.4.    Mission-Related Training. ............................................................................ 15

    2.5.    Mission Training:.......................................................................................... 15

|  |  |  |  |
|---|---|---|---|
|  | 2.6. | IQT for Senior Officers: | 15 |

**Chapter 3— MISSION QUALIFICATION AND CERTIFICATION TRAINING**                      **17**

|  |  |  |  |
|---|---|---|---|
|  | 3.1. | General. | 17 |
|  | 3.2. | Mission-Related Training: | 17 |
| Table | 3.1. | Mission-Related Training Requirements (T-3). | 17 |
|  | 3.3. | Initial Certification: | 18 |
|  | 3.4. | Mission Training: | 18 |
|  | 3.5. | MQT for Senior Officers: | 18 |
|  | 3.6. | Difference Training. | 19 |

**Chapter 4— CONTINUATION TRAINING**                                                              **20**

|  |  |  |  |
|---|---|---|---|
|  | 4.1. | General. | 20 |
|  | 4.2. | Crewmember Status. | 20 |
|  | 4.3. | Training Events/Tables. | 20 |
|  | 4.4. | Continuation Training Requirements. | 21 |
| Table | 4.1. | AFINC Crewmember Mission-Related CT Requirements. (T-3). | 21 |
|  | 4.5. | Specialized Mission Training. | 22 |
|  | 4.6. | Currencies, Recurrencies and Requalification. | 22 |
|  | 4.7. | Loss of Instructor Status and Requalification/Recurrency. | 22 |
|  | 4.8. | Regression. | 23 |
|  | 4.9. | End-of-Cycle Requirements. | 24 |
|  | 4.10. | Proration of Training. | 24 |
|  | 4.11. | Operational Missions. | 25 |
| Table | 4.2. | Proration Allowance. (T-3). | 25 |
|  | 4.12. | Regaining MR or BMC Status. | 25 |
| Figure | 4.1. | Regression Flow Chart. | 26 |

**Chapter 5— UPGRADE AND SPECIALIZED MISSION TRAINING**                            **27**

|  |  |  |  |
|---|---|---|---|
|  | 5.1. | General. | 27 |
|  | 5.2. | Requirements. | 27 |
|  | 5.3. | Instructor Upgrade. | 27 |

Attachment 1— GLOSSARY OF REFERENCES AND SUPPORTING INFORMATION          29

Attachment 2— GLOSSARY OF MISSION, SORTIE AND EVENT DEFINITIONS          34

Attachment 3— WHITE CARD SCENARIOS                                       38

Attachment 4— CYBERCREW RESOURCE MANAGEMENT                              39

## Chapter 1

## GENERAL INFORMATION

**1.1. Training Objectives.** This instruction prescribes basic policy and guidance for training United States Air Force Intranet Control (AFINC) crewmembers according to AFI 17-202V1.

1.1.1. The overall objective of the AFINC training program is to develop and maintain a high state of readiness for the immediate and effective employment across a full range of military operations. Mission readiness and effective employment are achieved through the development and mastery of core competencies for AFINC crewmembers.

1.1.2. The secondary objective is to standardize AFINC training requirements into a single source document.

**1.2. Abbreviations,** Acronyms and Terms. See Attachment 1.

1.2.1. For the purposes of this instruction, "certification" denotes a commander's action, whereas qualification denotes a formal Standardization and Evaluation (Stan/Eval).

1.2.2. Key words explained.

1.2.2.1. "Will" or "shall" indicates a mandatory requirement.

1.2.2.2. "Should" indicates a preferred, but not mandatory, method of accomplishment.

1.2.2.3. "May" indicates an acceptable or suggested means of accomplishment.

1.2.2.4. "Note" indicates operating procedures, techniques, etc., which are considered essential to emphasize.

**1.3. Responsibilities:**

1.3.1. Lead Command. Air Force Space Command (AFSPC) is designated lead command for the AFINC weapon system. The lead command is responsible for establishing and standardizing crewmember training requirements in coordination with user commands. AFSPC/A2/3/6 is authorized to manage all training course requirements and training tasks. AFSPC/A2/3/6 is the OPR for this AFI; AFSPC/A2/3/6 will:

1.3.1.1. Chair an annual Realistic Training Review Board (RTRB) to review training requirements and programs for AF cyber units. RTRB participants will include applicable AFSPC active and reserve component representatives. All AF units with assigned AFINC crewmembers will be invited to send representatives and inputs. **(T-2)**

1.3.1.2. Process all change requests for this instruction. **(T-2)**

1.3.2. All user MAJCOMs will:

1.3.2.1. Determine training requirements to fulfill primary (and secondary, if applicable) Designed Operational Capability (DOC) statement missions as well as meet unit tasking.

1.3.2.2. Submit MAJCOM supplements to HQ USAF AF/A3CX/A6CX, through HQ AFSPC/A2/3/6T, for approval during topline coordination of the document. Copies of approved and published supplements will be provided by the issuing office to HQ USAF

AF/A3C/A6C, HQ AFSPC/A2/3/6T, and applicable MAJCOM offices of primary responsibility (OPR).

1.3.2.3. Publish annual AFINC Ready Cybercrew Program (RCP) Ready Training Memorandum (RTM).

1.3.2.4. Review subordinate unit supplemental instructions and training programs annually.

1.3.3. Wings and groups will:

1.3.3.1. Develop programs to ensure training objectives are met. The primary training priority should be to train all designated crewmembers to Mission Ready (MR) status. Assist subordinate squadrons in management of training programs, ensure programs meet unit needs, and provide necessary staff support. AFSPC wing/groups will assist AFRC unit training programs as required or requested IAW applicable unit support programs, memorandums of agreement, or memorandums of understanding. **(T-3)**

1.3.3.2. Attach Crewmember Position Indicator (CPI)-6/-8/-B/-D personnel to an operational squadron. See Attachment 4 for CPI explanation and definitions. **(T-3)**

1.3.3.3. Except when otherwise mandated, designate the training level to which each CPI–6/-8/-B/-D will train. Upon request, provide AFSPC/A2/3/6T (through MAJCOM/A3T or equivalent) with a list of MR and Basic Mission Capable (BMC) manning positions. Review programs and manning position designations annually. **(T-3)**

1.3.3.4. Develop additional training requirements and/or programs necessary to meet unit mission requirements. Units may include these requirements in local training procedures. **(T-3)**

1.3.4. Squadrons. The SQ/CC primary training priority should be to train all designated crewmembers to MR or BMC. Squadron supervision will: **(T-3)**

1.3.4.1. Squadron Training, the Unit Training Office (DOT) function is responsible for maintaining training forms and unit certification documents for all squadron personnel and personnel attached to the squadron for cyberspace operations. **(T-3)**

1.3.4.2. Unit Stan/Eval will maintain the letter of certification (i.e., letter of Xs) summarizing crewmember certifications; this letter will be signed by the OG/CC, SQ/CC or SQ/DO and may be maintained via electronic storage. **(T-3)**

1.3.4.3. Ensure adequate continuity and supervision of individual training needs, experience and proficiencies of assigned and attached crewmembers. **(T-3)**

1.3.4.4. Ensure review of training and evaluation records of newly assigned crewmembers and those completing formal training to determine the training required for them to achieve BMC or MR status and to ensure provisions of this volume are met. **(T-3)**

1.3.4.5. Ensure Ready Cybercrew Program (RCP) missions are oriented towards maintaining mission ready proficiency and tactical employment. Provide guidance to ensure only effective RCP missions are logged. **(T-3)**

1.3.4.6. Determine missions and events in which individual MR crewmembers will maintain MR certification/qualification. **(T-3)**

1.3.4.7. Determine missions and events in which individual BMC crewmembers will maintain basic certification/qualification. **(T-3)**

1.3.4.8. Determine utilization of BMC crewmembers. **(T-3)**

1.3.4.9. Determine how many and which crewmembers will carry special certifications (mission commander, etc.,) and qualifications (instructor, etc.). **(T-3)**

1.3.4.10. Assist the wing or group in the development of the unit training programs. **(T-3)**

1.3.4.11. Monitor individual assigned and attached crewmembers currencies, proficiencies, and requirements. **(T-3)**

1.3.4.12. Ensure crewmembers participate only in sorties, missions, events, and tasks for which they are qualified/certified and adequately prepared, trained, and current. **(T-3)**

1.3.4.13. Ensure flight commanders or designated representatives monitor quality of training, identify training deficiencies, and advise SQ/CC of additional training needs. **(T-3)**

1.3.4.14. Execute unit-level crewmembers certifications described in this instruction. **(T-3)**

1.3.5. Individual crewmembers will:  **(T-3)**

1.3.5.1. Be responsible for monitoring and completing all training requirements. **(T-3)**

1.3.5.2. Ensure they participate only in operational activities for which they are qualified/certified, current, and prepared. **(T-3)**

**1.4. Training** . Cybercrew training is designed to progress an individual from Initial Qualification Training (IQT), through Mission Qualification Training (MQT), to annual Continuation Training (CT). Requalification training (RT), upgrade training, and instructor training are additional training requirements for AFINC employment.

1.4.1. Initial Qualification Training (IQT). Training needed to qualify for basic crewmember duties in an assigned crew position for a specific weapon system, without regard to the unit's operational mission. See **Chapter 2**. **(T-3)**

1.4.2. Mission Qualification Training (MQT). The purpose of MQT is to qualify crewmembers in assigned crew positions to perform the command or unit mission IAW the unit's DOC statement. See **Chapter 3**. **(T-3)**

1.4.3. Continuation Training (CT). The CT program provides crewmembers with the volume, frequency, and mix of training necessary to maintain proficiency in the assigned certification/qualification level.

1.4.3.1. Ready Cybercrew Program (RCP). RCP is the CT program designed to focus training on capabilities needed to accomplish a unit's core tasked missions and fulfill DOC statement mission requirements. Upon completion of IQT and MQT, crewmembers will have received training in all the basic mission-sets of the unit. After MQT completion, crewmembers will then be assigned to a MR or BMC crew position within the unit and maintain the appropriate level of proficiency and currency per the RCP tasking memorandum. **(T-3)**

1.4.4. Requalification Training (RT). RT is designed to provide the training necessary to requalify a crewmembers member with an expired qualification evaluation or loss of currency exceeding 6 months (for currency items specified in Chapter 4). **(T-3)**

1.4.5. Mission Ready (MR). A crewmember who satisfactorily completed IQT and MQT, and maintains qualification and proficiency in the unit mission.

1.4.5.1. All CPI-1/-2/-A/-Z designated positions will maintain certification/qualification status. The OG/CC may require other Cybercrew Position Indicator (CPI)-6/B positions not assigned to the squadron to be certified/qualified. See Attachment 4 for CPI explanation and definitions. **(T-3)**

1.4.5.2. MR crewmembers will maintain currencies that affect MR status, accomplish all core designated training (missions and events), and all mission related training. Failure to complete required MR training or maintain currencies will result in regression to BMC. Failure of an MR crewmember to maintain BMC currencies will result in regression to non-MR (NMR) status. MR crewmembers, regressed to BMC, may perform missions and events in which they are certified at the discretion of the SQ/CC. **(T-3)**

1.4.6. Basic Mission Capable (BMC). A crewmember who satisfactorily completed IQT and MQT, is qualified in some aspect of the unit mission, but does not maintain MR status. The crewmember must be able to attain full MR status as specified in MAJCOM-provided guidance. **(T-3)**

1.4.6.1. BMC-coded positions are assigned to crewmembers with the primary job of performing wing supervision or staff functions that directly support cyber operations (e.g., numbered air force staff, wing staff, OSS personnel, etc.). **(T-3)**

1.4.6.2. Active Duty BMC crewmembers and activated ARC BMC crewmembers must be able to attain MR status and, if required, certification/qualification in 30 days (respectively). **(T-2)**

1.4.6.3. BMC crewmembers accomplish all mission related training designated by the RTM. **(T-2)**

1.4.6.4. BMC crewmembers may participate in any real-world mission in which they are current, proficient, and certified/qualified, without any additional training, with the supervision of an instructor as determined by the SQ/CC. **(T-3)**

1.4.6.5. Failure to complete required BMC training will result in regression to non-BMC (N-BMC) status. While N-BMC, SQ/CC will determine missions the crewmembers may perform and ensure an instructor supervises the member during real-world mission. **(T-3)**

**1.5. Training Concepts and Policies:**

1.5.1. Units will design training programs to achieve the highest degree of readiness consistent with safety and resource availability. Training must balance the need for realism against the expected threat, crew capabilities, and safety. This volume provides training guidelines and polices for use with operational procedures specified in applicable operational publications.

1.5.2. Design training to achieve mission capability in squadron-tasked roles, maintain proficiency, and enhance mission accomplishment and safety. RCP training missions should emphasize either live network operations or training scenarios that reflect procedures and operations based on employment plans, location, current intelligence, and opposition capabilities. Use of Tactics, Tips and Procedures (TTP's) applicable to mission scenarios are desired. **(T-2)**

1.5.3. Unless specifically directed, the SQ/CC determines the level of supervision necessary to accomplish the required training. An instructor is required if mission objectives include introduction to new or modified tasks and/or instruction to correct previous discrepancies. **(T-3)**

**1.6. Experienced Crewmember Requirements.** AFINC operators are declared experienced on the weapon system when they meet the requirements in Table 1.1. **(T-3)**

**Table 1.1.  Experienced Crewmember Requirements (T-3).**

| Position | Declared Experienced (Hours) | SMQ Experience Declaration (Operator + SMQ hours aggregate) * See Note 1 | Instructor Eligible (Hours) |
|---|---|---|---|
| AFINC Operator | 360 | NA | 360 |
| Operator-Router (SMQ) | 630 | 990 total hours (min 630 SMQ) | 990 |
| Operator-DNS/MEG (SMQ) | 480 | 900 total hours (min 480 SMQ) | 900 |
| Operator-Net Sec (SMQ) | 540 | 960 total hours (min 540 SMQ) | 960 |
| Operator-Analyst (SMQ) | 960 | 2160 min total sorties (min 960 hours SMQ & min requirements from 2 other SMQ positions) | 2160 |
| AFINC Operations Controller | 480 | 840 total hours (min 480 Ops Controller) | 840 sorties |
| AFINC Crew Commander | 630 | 990 total hours (min 630 Crew Commander) | 990 sorties |

Notes:
1.  SMQ experience = Operator (360 hours) + SMQ (e.g., 300 hours)

**1.7.  RCP Policy and Management:**

1.7.1. The RCP training cycle is 12 months in duration, begins each fiscal year and is executed IAW the RTM. Each RCP status (i.e., MR or BMC) is defined by a total number of RCP missions, events, and associated currencies determined by HHQ guidance and unit commanders. **(T-3)**

1.7.2. Total number of missions and events for MR or BMC is the primary factor for maintaining an individual's RCP status. Failure to accomplish all training requirements may lead to an individual's regression by the SQ/CC, IAW HHQ guidance. **(T-3)**

1.7.3. Logging of an effective RCP mission requires accomplishing a tactical mission or training mission, and completion of the RCP mission/events. **(T-3)**

1.7.4. For RCP, non-effective sorties are logged and reported when a sortie is planned and started, but a majority of valid training for that type of mission is not accomplished due to system malfunction, power failures, etc. **(T-3)**

1.7.5. Progression from BMC to MR requires: **(T-2)**

1.7.5.1. A 1-month lookback at the MR mission rate. **(T-3)**

1.7.5.2. Certification/qualification in all core missions and events required at MR. **(T-3)**

1.7.5.3. Confirmation the progressed crewmember can complete the prorated number of mission and event requirements remaining at MR by the end of the training cycle. **(T-3)**

1.7.5.4. Completion of mission-related training, to include a current certification as applicable to the assigned unit's Designated Operational Capability (DOC) statement. **(T-3)**

1.7.6. MR and BMC crewmember will complete the required monthly mission rate. If unable, refer to Regression, paragraph 4.9. **(T-3)**

1.7.7. End of cycle training requirements are based on the crewmember's experience level, as outlined in paragraph 1.7, on the last day of the current training cycle. **(T-3)**

**1.8. Training Mission Program Development:**

1.8.1. RTM MR or BMC mission and event requirements apply to all MR and BMC crewmembers, as well as those carrying special mission certifications/qualifications (see Attachment 2). The standard mission requirements listed in the RTM establish the minimum number of missions per training cycle for MR and BMC levels of training. The RTM takes precedence over this volume and may contain updated requirements, missions, events, or tasks not yet incorporated into Attachment 2. The RTM applies to all AFINC crewmembers. **(T-3)**

**1.9. Training Records and Reports:**

1.9.1. Units will maintain crewmember records for individual training and evaluations IAW:

1.9.1.1. AFI 17-202V1

1.9.1.2. AFI 17-202V2, *Cybercrew Standardization & Evaluation*

1.9.1.3. Any additional Higher Headquarter (HHQ) supplement to the above mentioned volumes.

1.9.2. Track the following information for all crewmembers (as applicable):

1.9.2.1. Mission-related training (e.g., tactics training, crew resource management training, etc.). **(T-3)**

1.9.2.2. Requirements and accomplishment of individual sorties, mission types, and events cumulatively for the training cycle. **(T-3)**

1.9.2.3. RCP mission requirements and accomplishment using 1-month and 3-month running totals for lookback commensurate with CT status (MR or BMC). **(T-3)**

1.9.2.3.1. One-Month Sortie Lookback: Total individual RCP sorties that are tracked for a 30-day time period. This lookback is used to assess individual progress in achieving the Total Sorties (minimum) required for the 12-month training cycle. **(T-3)**

1.9.2.3.2. Three-Month Sortie Lookback: This lookback is used to assess individual progress in achieving the Total Sorties (minimum) required for the 12-month training cycle. **(T-3)**

1.9.2.3.3. ARC will use 3 month lookbacks. **(T-3)**

## 1.10. Crewmember Utilization Policy:

1.10.1. Commanders will ensure wing/group crewmember (CPI-1/-2/-A) fill authorized positions IAW Unit Manning Documents (UMD) and that crewmember status is properly designated (see Attachment 4 for CPI explanation and definitions). The overall objective is for crewmembers to perform mission-related duties. Supervisors may assign crewmember to valid, short-term tasks (escort officer, operational review board (ORB), etc.,) but must continually weigh the factors involved, such as level of crewmember tasking, proficiency, currency, and experience. For inexperienced crewmember in the first year of their initial operational assignment, supervisors should limit non-crew duties to those related to unit mission activities. **(T-3)**

## 1.11. Sortie Allocation and Unit Manpower Guidance:

1.11.1. In general, an inexperienced CPI-1/-2/-A/-Z crewmember should receive priority over experienced crewmember. **(T-3)**

1.11.2. There is no maximum sortie requirement for MR crewmember. The RCP Tasking Memorandum (RTM) defines the minimum sortie requirements for crewmembers per training cycle. **(T-3)**

**1.12. Training on Operational Missions.** Unless specifically prohibited or restricted by weapons system operating procedures, specific theater operations order (OPORD), or specific higher-headquarter (HHQ) guidance, the OG/CC exercising operational control may approve upgrade, certification/qualification, or special certification/qualification training on operational missions. In order to maximize efficient utilization of training resources, units will take maximum advantage of opportunities to conduct appropriate CT items that may be conveniently suited to concurrent operational mission segments. **(T-3)**

## 1.13. In-Unit Training Time Limitations:

1.13.1. Comply with the time limitations in Table 1.2. Crewmembers entered in an in-unit training program leading to qualification, requalification, or certification will be dedicated to that training program. **(T-2)**

1.13.2. Training time start date is the date when the first significant training event (a training event directly contributing to qualification, certification, or upgrade) has begun, or 45-days (90 days ARC) after being attached or assigned to the unit after completion of the formal school; whichever occurs first. Training time ends with the syllabus completion. **(T-3)**

1.13.3. If member is projected to exceed the training cycle, units will notify the OG/CC (or equivalent) in writing before the crewmember exceeds upgrade training time limits in Table 1.2. SQ/CCs may extend listed training times up to 60 days (120 days ARC) provided appropriate justification is documented in the crewmember's training folder. **(T-3)**

1.13.3.1. Include training difficulty, unit corrective action to resolve and prevent recurrence, and estimated completion date. **(T-3)**

**Table 1.2. In-Unit Training Time Limitations Active Duty (Calendar Days). (T-3).**

| Training | Crew Commander | Operations Controller | Operator | Notes |
|---|---|---|---|---|
| Mission Qualification Training | N/A | N/A | 90 | 1,3 |
| Requalification | 45 | 45 | 45 | 1,3 |
| Certification | 30 | 30 | 30 | 1,3 |
| Instructor Upgrade | 45 | 45 | 45 | 1,3 |
| Special Mission Upgrade | N/A | N/A | 90 | 1,3 |
| Upgrade Training | 90 | 90 | N/A | 1,3 |
| BMC to MR | 30 | 30 | 30 | 1, 2,3 |
| *Notes:* | | | | |
| 1. Training time begins with the first training event | | | | |
| 2. BMC crewmember must be able to attain MR status and, if required, certification / qualification in 30 days or less for those missions/events that they maintain familiarization only | | | | |
| 3. 180 days for non-full time ARC/ANG members | | | | |

**1.14. Periodic and End-of-Cycle Training Reports.** Unless directed otherwise, will be in accordance with MAJCOM continuation training/reporting guidance.

**1.15. Waiver Authority:**

1.15.1. Waivers. Unless another approval authority is cited ("T-0, T-1, T-2, T-3"), waiver authority for this volume is the MAJCOM/A3 (or equivalent). Submit requests for waivers using AF Form 679 through the chain of command to the appropriate Tier waiver approval authority. If approved, waivers remain in effect for the life of the published guidance, unless the waiver authority specifies a shorter period of time, cancels in writing, or issues a change that alters the basis for the waiver.

1.15.2. With MAJCOM/A3 (or equivalent) approval, waiver authority for all requirements of the RTM is the OG/CC. Additional guidance may be provided in the memo. Unless specifically noted otherwise in the appropriate section, and also with MAJCOM/A3 (or equivalent) approval, the OG/CC may adjust individual requirements in Chapter 4 and Chapter 5, on a case-by-case basis, to accommodate variations in crewmember experience and performance. **(T-2)**

1.15.3. Formal School Training and Prerequisites. Any planned exception to a formal course syllabus (or prerequisite) requires a syllabus waiver. Submit waiver request through MAJCOM/A3T (or equivalent) to the waiver authority listed in the course syllabus. If required for units' designated mission, events waived or not accomplished at the formal school will be accomplished in-unit before assigning MR status. **(T-2)**

1.15.4. In-Unit Training Waiver. MAJCOM/A3T (or equivalent) is approval/waiver authority for in-unit training to include syllabus and prerequisite waivers. Before approval, review the appropriate syllabus and consider availability of formal instruction and requirements. All in-unit training will utilize formal courseware in accordance with AFI 17-

202V1. MAJCOMs will coordinate with the Formal Training Unit (FTU) to arrange courseware delivery to the unit for in-unit training. **(T-2)**

1.15.5. Waiver authority for supplemental guidance will be as specified in the supplement and approved through higher level coordination authority. **(T-2)**

1.15.6. Units subordinate to a NAF will forward requests through the NAF/A3T (or equivalent) to the MAJCOM/A3T (or equivalent). Waivers from other than the MAJCOM/A3 (or equivalent) will include the appropriate MAJCOM/A3 (or equivalent) as an information addressee. **(T-2)**

## Chapter 2

## INITIAL QUALIFICATION TRAINING

**2.1. General.** This chapter outlines AFINC IQT requirements for all crewmembers.

**2.2. Formal Training.** AFINC IQT includes training that will normally be conducted during formal syllabus courses at the FTU.

**2.3. Local Training.** In circumstances when FTU training is not available within a reasonable time period, local IQT may be performed at the unit IAW the provisions of this chapter. Local IQT will be conducted using appropriate formal training course syllabus and requirements. When local IQT is authorized, the gaining unit assumes responsibility for the burden of providing this training. **(T-2)**

2.3.1. Requests to conduct local IQT will be sent to the MAJCOM for approval.

2.3.2. Requests to conduct local IQT will include the following:

2.3.2.1. Justification for the local training in lieu of FTU training. **(T-2)**

2.3.2.2. Summary of individual's mission related experience, to include dates. **(T-2)**

2.3.2.3. Date training will begin and expected completion date. **(T-2)**

2.3.2.4. Requested exceptions to formal course syllabus, with rationale. **(T-2)**

**2.4. Mission-Related Training.** Current and available reference materials, such as AFTTP 3-1.AFINC, other applicable AFTTP 3-1s and 3-3s, unit guides, and other available training material and programs, will be used as supporting materials to the maximum extent possible. **(T-2)**

**2.5. Mission Training:**

2.5.1. Mission sequence and prerequisites will be IAW the appropriate formal course syllabus (unless waived). **(T-2)**

2.5.2. Training will be completed within the time specified by the syllabus. Failure to complete within the specified time limit requires notification through channels to MAJCOM/A3 with crewmember member's name, rank, reason for delay, planned actions, and estimated completion date. **(T-2)**

2.5.3. Crewmember in IQT will train under the appropriate supervision as annotated in the formal course syllabus until completing the QUAL evaluation. **(T-2)**

2.5.4. Formal course syllabus mission objectives and tasks are minimum requirements for IQT. However, additional training events, based on student proficiency and background, may be incorporated into the IQT program with SQ/CC authorization. Additional training due to student non-progression is available within the constraints of the formal course syllabus and may be added at SQ/CC discretion. **(T-3)**

**2.6. IQT for Senior Officers:**

2.6.1. All senior officer training (colonel selects and above) will be conducted at the FTUs unless waived IAW AFI 17-202V1. **(T-2)**

2.6.2. Senior officers must meet course entry prerequisites and will complete all syllabus requirements unless waived IAW AFI 17-202V1. **(T-2)**

2.6.3. If senior officers are trained at the base to which they are assigned they will be considered in a formal training status for the duration of the course. Their duties will be turned over to appropriate CDs or CVs until training is completed. Waiver authority for this paragraph is MAJCOM/CC (submitted through MAJCOM/A3). **(T-2)**

**Chapter 3**

**MISSION QUALIFICATION AND CERTIFICATION TRAINING**

**3.1. General.** MQT is a unit-developed training program that upgrades IQT-complete crewmember to BMC or MR status to accomplish the unit DOC statement missions. Guidance in this chapter, which represents the minimum, is provided to assist SQ/CCs in developing their MQT program, which must have OG/CC approval prior to use. Squadrons may further tailor their program for individual crewmember, based on current qualifications (e.g., USAFWS graduate, Instructor), certifications (e.g., MC, DCC, Stan/Eval), experience, currency, documented performance, and formal training. Squadrons may use applicable portions of MQT to create a recertification program for crewmember that have regressed from MR to BMC status. **(T-3)**

3.1.1. MQT will be completed within 90 calendar days (180 days for ARC) starting from the day after completion of IQT or the crewmember's first duty day in the gaining unit if IQT was completed prior to arrival. If the crewmember elects to take leave prior to being entered into MQT, the timing will begin after the termination of the leave. Training is complete upon SQ/CC certification of MR or BMC status (subsequent to the successful completion of the MQT MSN qualification evaluation). Notify MAJCOM/A3T (through MAJCOM/A3TT or equivalent) either if training exceed the 90-day time period or there is a delay beginning MQT (e.g., due to security clearance) that exceeds 30 days (90 days for ARC). **(T-3)**

**3.2. Mission-Related Training:**

3.2.1. Units will develop blocks of instruction covering areas pertinent to the mission as determined by the SQ/CC. Training accomplished during IQT may be credited towards this requirement. **(T-3)**

3.2.2. Mission-related training may be tailored to the individual's background and experience or particular local conditions. Current and available reference materials, such as AFTTP 3-1.AFINC, other applicable AFTTP 3-1s and 3-3s, unit guides, and other available training material and programs, will be used as supporting materials to the maximum extent possible. **(T-3)**

**Table 3.1. Mission-Related Training Requirements (T-3).**

| Code | Event | Crew Position | Notes |
|------|-------|---------------|-------|
| GTR001 | Unit Indoctrination Training | All | 1 |
| GTR002 | Weapons and Tactics | All | 1 |
| GTR003 | Risk Management | All | 1, 2 |
| 1. Accomplish upon arrival after each permanent change of station (PCS). See Attachment 2 for event description. 2. Previously trained crewmembers transferring between units need to re-accomplish this event if they have lost currency or as determined by the SQ/CC. | | | |

3.2.3. Mission-related training will be built to support the mission and concept of operations of the individual squadron; incorporate appropriate portions of AFTTP 3-1.AFINC and other mission-related documents. **(T-3)**

**3.3. Initial Certification:**

3.3.1. Initial Certification of MR crewmembers will be completed within 30 days after completing MQT (recommended, but not required for BMC crewmember). Failure to comply will result in regression to NMR until complete. Suggested briefing guides are at Attachment 3. **(T-3)**

**3.4. Mission Training:**

3.4.1. Supervision. A squadron instructor is required for all training missions unless specified otherwise. **(T-3)**

3.4.2. Minimum Sortie Requirements. The minimum sorties required in a local MQT program will be IAW the MQT course syllabus (not required if portions of the MQT program are used to recertify crewmembers that have regressed from MR to BMC). Reference the paragraphs below for further details and recommended sortie flows the SQ/CC may use to develop the unit's MQT program. **(T-3)**

3.4.3. Mission sequence and prerequisites will be IAW the appropriate unit MQT course syllabus (unless waived). **(T-2)**

3.4.4. Mission Objectives: Be familiar with local area requirements and procedures. Specific Mission Tasks: local area familiarization, emergency procedures, and other tasks determined by the unit. **(T-3)**

3.4.5. Individual events may be accomplished anytime during MQT, however all events will be accomplished prior to SQ/CC certification of MR or BMC status. **(T-3)**

3.4.6. Mission Types. AFINC mission types are defined in current SPINS.

   3.4.6.1. Reference standing SPINS for mission type definitions.

3.4.7. Training will be completed within the time specified by the syllabus. Failure to complete training within the specified time limit requires notification through channels to the MAJCOM/A3T with crewmember's name, rank, reason for delay, planned actions, and estimated completion date. **(T-2)**

3.4.8. Crewmembers in MQT will train under the appropriate supervision as annotated in the formal course syllabus until completing the qualification evaluation. **(T-3)**

3.4.9. Formal course syllabus mission objectives and tasks are minimum requirements for IQT. However, additional training events, based on student proficiency and background, may be incorporated into the IQT program with SQ/CC authorization. Additional training due to student non-progression is available within the constraints of the formal course syllabus and may be added at SQ/CC discretion. **(T-3)**

**3.5. MQT for Senior Officers:**

3.5.1. All senior officer training (colonel selects and above) will be conducted at the unit. **(T-2)**

3.5.2. Senior officers must meet course entry prerequisites and will complete all syllabus requirements unless waived by the MAJCOM/A3. **(T-2)**

3.5.3. Senior officers will be considered in a formal training status for the duration of the course. Their duties will be turned over to appropriate CDs or CVs until training is completed. Waiver authority for this paragraph is the MAJCOM/CC (submitted through the MAJCOM/A3). **(T-2)**

**3.6. Difference Training.** When Difference Training is required, DOT will need to update IQT and MQT and provide training to all crewmembers. Training will be documented IAW AFI 17-202V1. Difference Training does not disqualify members from MR status. However, all untrained members cannot perform tasks associated with the new guidance until trained, unless under the supervision of an instructor/evaluator. New training and procedures should be reviewed immediately following the initial training session and updated; then updated a second time by end of the following quarter. **(T-2)**

**Chapter 4**

**CONTINUATION TRAINING**

**4.1. General.** This chapter establishes the minimum crewmember training requirements to maintain MR or BMC status for an assigned training status. The SQ/CC will ensure each crewmember receives sufficient training to maintain individual proficiency **(T-3)**.

**4.2. Crewmember Status.** SQ/CCs will assign AFINC crewmembers a status using the following criteria:

4.2.1. Mission Ready (MR). For SORTS, a crewmember member who satisfactorily completed IQT and MQT, and maintains qualification, certification, currency and proficiency in the command or unit operational mission.

4.2.1.1. The crewmember shall be able to attain full unit mission certification to meet operational tasking within 30 days. **(T-2)**

4.2.2. Non-Mission Ready (NMR). A crewmember that is unqualified, non-current or incomplete in required continuation training, or not certified to perform the unit mission. **(T-3)**

4.2.3. MR and BMC crewmembers will accomplish and/or maintain RCP requirements, for their respective status, and the appropriate events in the RCP tables in this Instruction and the RTM. **(T-3)**

4.2.4. Operators will maintain all required certifications to operate on the network or will be subject to decertification if those requirements are not met. **(T-3)**

**4.3. Training Events/Tables.** Standardized training events identifiers and descriptions are located in Attachment 2. Units will include unit-specific events comprising a description in their local training documentation. **(T-3)**

4.3.1. Crediting Event Accomplishment. Credit events accomplished on training, operational missions and satisfactory evaluations or certifications toward RCP requirements and establish a subsequent due date. Use the date of successful evaluation as the date of accomplishment for all mission-related training events that were trained during a formal course. A successful evaluation establishes a new current and qualified reference date for all accomplished events. For IQT or requalification training, numbers of events accomplished prior to the evaluation are not credited to any crew position. In all cases, numbers of events successfully accomplished during the evaluation or certification are credited toward the crew position. **(T-3)**

4.3.2. For an unsatisfactory evaluation, do not log CT requirements for those events graded U/Q3 (according to AFI 17-202V2) until re-qualified. **(T-3)**

4.3.3. Instructors and evaluators may credit up to 50 percent of their total CT requirements while instructing or evaluating. **(T-3)**

**4.4. Continuation Training Requirements.** Completion and tracking of continuation training is ultimately the responsibility of the individual crewmember. Crewmembers should actively work with their supervisors, unit schedulers and training offices to ensure accomplishment of their continuation training requirements. Crewmembers attached to units are responsible for reporting accomplished training event to their attached unit. **(T-3)**

4.4.1. Mission-Related Training Events. Crewmembers will comply with requirements of Table 4.1. Failure to accomplish events in Table 4.1 leads to NMR status. **(T-3)**

4.4.1.1. Weapons and Tactics Academic Training. Units will establish a weapons and tactics academic training program to satisfy MQT and CT requirements. Training is required semi-annually during each training cycle. SQ/CCs will provide guidance to unit weapons shops to ensure all crewmember are informed/reminded of new/current AFINC systems, and mission-specific TTP. **(T-3)**

4.4.1.1.1. Academic instructors will be Weapons Instructor Course (WIC) graduates or have attended the applicable academic portion(s) of school, if possible. **(T-3)**

4.4.1.1.2. Instruction should include (as applicable), but is not limited to: **(T-3)**

4.4.1.1.2.1. Applicable AF Tactics, Techniques, and Procedures (AFTTP) 3-1 & 3-3 series publications, AFI 17-2, *Air Force Intranet Network Control (AFINC) Operations and Procedures, Volume 3* (AFI 17-2 AFNICV3) and other documents pertaining to the execution of the unit's mission. **(T-3)**

4.4.1.1.2.2. Specialized training to support specific weapons, tactics, mission capabilities, rules of engagement (ROE), and other mission related activities. **(T-3)**

4.4.1.2. Risk Management (RM). Crewmember will participate in RM training once every training cycle. Briefings will include the concepts outlined in AFPAM 90-803, *Risk Management (RM) Guidelines and Tools*. RM training will be tracked. Failure to complete RM training will result in NMR status. **(T-3)**

**Table 4.1.  AFINC Crewmember Mission-Related CT Requirements. (T-3).**

| Code | Event | Position | Frequency | Notes |
|---|---|---|---|---|
| GTR001 | Weapons & Tactics | All | 179d | 1, 2 |
| | | | | |
| GTR003 | Risk Management | All | 365d | 1, 2 |

*Notes:*
1. "d" is the maximum number of days between events.
2. Failure to complete this event within the time prescribed leads to NMR status. Crewmembers will not be able to accomplish unsupervised crew duties until the delinquent event is accomplished or waived.

4.4.2. Mission Training Events. Crewmembers will comply with requirements of the RCP Tasking Memorandum (RTM) for their respective position. Total sorties and events are minimums which ensure training to continually meet all DOC tasked requirements and may not be reduced except in proration/waiver. Unless specifically noted the OG/CC is the waiver authority for all RCP requirements and for all provisions in Chapter 4 and Chapter 5 of this volume. Failure to accomplish events in these tables may lead to NMR status. **(T-3)**

**4.5. Specialized Mission Training.** Specialized Mission Training is any special skills necessary to carry out the unit's assigned mission that is not required by every crewmember member. Specialized Mission Training consists of upgrade training such as special mission qualification (SMQ), instructor upgrade, etc. Specialized training is normally accomplished after a crewmember is assigned MR or BMC status. Unless otherwise specified, crewmembers in MR or BMC positions may hold special mission certifications as long as additional training requirements are accomplished. (See Chapter 5) **(T-3)**

4.5.1. The SQ/CC will determine which crewmembers will train for and maintain special mission qualifications and certifications. **(T-3)**

**4.6. Currencies, Recurrencies and Requalification.**

4.6.1. Currency. The RTM defines currency requirements for MR and BMC crewmembers. Crewmembers may not instruct, evaluate or perform any event in which they are not qualified and current unless under instructor supervision. Currency may be established or updated by:

4.6.1.1. Accomplishing the event as a qualified crewmember provided member's currency has not expired. **(T-3)**

4.6.1.2. Accomplishing the event as a qualified crewmember under supervision of a current instructor. **(T-3)**

4.6.1.3. Events satisfactorily performed on any evaluation may be used to establish or update currency in that event. **(T-3)**

4.6.1.4. If a crewmember loses a currency, thereby requiring recurrency, that mission or event may not be performed except for the purpose of regaining currency. Non-current events must be satisfied before the crewmember is considered certified/qualified (as applicable) to perform those events unsupervised. Loss of currencies affecting MR status will require regression to BMC (see paragraph 4.9); loss of currencies not affecting MR status does not require regression. **(T-3)**

**4.7. Loss of Instructor Status and Requalification/Recurrency.** Instructors may lose instructor status for the following:

4.7.1. Loss of currency for greater than 180 days. **(T-3)**

4.7.2. They become noncurrent in a mission or event which causes removal from MR or BMC status and the SQ/CC deems that loss of currency is of sufficient importance to require complete decertification (but not a complete loss of qualification). **(T-3)**

4.7.3. As long as the affected crewmember retains instructor qualification IAW AFI 17-202V2, recertification will be at the SQ/CC's discretion. **(T-3)**

4.7.3.1. If the SQ/CC does not elect to decertify the individual or if the individual becomes noncurrent in missions or events which do not require removal from MR or BMC status, instructor status may be retained, but the instructor will not instruct that mission or event until the required currency is regained. **(T-3)**

4.7.4. Instructor Lack of Ability. Instructors serve solely at the discretion of the SQ/CC. Instructors should exemplify a higher level of performance and present themselves as reliable and authoritative experts in their respective duty positions. Instructors exhibiting substandard performance should be reviewed for suitability of continued instructor duty. Instructors will be decertified if:

4.7.4.1. Awarded an unsatisfactory grade in any area of the evaluation. **(T-3)**

4.7.4.2. Failure of a qualification. **(T-3)**

4.7.4.3. SQ/CC deems instructor is substandard, ineffective, or providing incorrect procedures, techniques, or policy guidance. **(T-3)**

4.7.4.4. Decertified instructors may regain instructor status by correcting applicable deficiency and completing the training and/or evaluation as specified by the SQ/CC. **(T-3)**

**4.8. Regression.**

4.8.1. MR or BMC Regression for Failure to Meet Lookback. Only RCP training missions and cyberspace operations sorties may be used for lookback. If the crewmember does not meet lookback requirements throughout the training cycle, SQ/CC can regress the crewmember from MR to BMC or NMR. **(T-3)**

4.8.1.1. Failure to meet 3 month lookback requires a review of the crewmember's 3-month sortie history. If the 3-month lookback was met, the crewmember may, at SQ/CC discretion, remain in MR or BMC status. Failure to meet the 3-month lookback will result in regression to BMC or NMR/N-BMC, as applicable, or the crewmember may be placed in supervised status at the SQ/CC's discretion. If probation is chosen, the only way to remove a crewmember from probation and preserve the current status is to reestablish a 1-month lookback at the end of the probation period (not applicable to ARC). **(T-3)**

4.8.1.2. Lookback computations begin following completion of MQT. The crewmember must maintain 1-month lookback until a 3-month lookback is possible (not applicable to ARC). SQ/CCs may apply supervisory rules as described in paragraph 4.9.1.1 if a new MR or BMC crewmember fails to meet currency and proficiency requirements during the 1-month lookback while establishing 3-month lookback. In addition, 1-month lookback will start the first full month of MR or BMC status. **(T-3)**

4.8.2. Regression for Failed Evaluations. Crewmembers who fail a periodic evaluation are unqualified and will regress to NMR as applicable. Crewmembers will remain NMR until successfully completing required corrective action, re-evaluation, and are re-certified by the SQ/CC. **(T-3)**

4.8.3. Failure to Maintain Standards. If a qualified crewmember demonstrates lack of proficiency or knowledge the SQ/CC may elect to regress the individual to NMR as applicable. These crewmembers will remain NMR until successful completion of corrective action as determined by the SQ/CC, an evaluation if required and are re-certified by the SQ/CC. **(T-3)**

**4.9. End-of-Cycle Requirements.** Crewmembers who fail to complete mission or event requirements by the end of training cycle may require additional training depending on the type and magnitude of the deficiency. Refer to paragraph 4.11 for proration guidance. In all cases, units will report training shortfalls to the OG/CC. **(T-3)**

4.9.1. Crewmembers failing to meet annual RCP events or minimum total sortie requirements may continue CT at MR or BMC as determined by lookback. The SQ/CC will determine if additional training is required. **(T-3)**

4.9.2. Failure to meet specific MR or BMC mission type requirements will result in one of the following: **(T-3)**

4.9.2.1. Regression to NMR if the SQ/CC determines the mission type deficiency is significant. To regain MR or BMC status, the crewmember will complete all deficient mission types. These missions may also be counted toward the total requirements for the new training cycle. **(T-3)**

4.9.2.2. Continuation at MR or BMC status if total RCP missions and lookback are maintained and the mission type deficiencies are deemed insignificant by the SQ/CC. The SQ/CC will determine if any additional training is required to address shortfall. **(T-3)**

4.9.3. Failure to accomplish missions/events required for Special Mission capabilities or certifications/qualifications will result in loss of that certification/qualification. The SQ/CC will determine recertification requirements. Requalification requirements are IAW AFI 17-202V2 applicable HHQ guidance, and AFI 17-2AFINCv2. **(T-3)**

**4.10. Proration of Training.**

4.10.1. Proration of End-of-Cycle Requirements. At the end of the training cycle the SQ/CC may prorate any training requirements precluded by the following events: initial arrival date in squadron, emergency leave, non-mission TDYs, exercises, or deployments. Ordinary annual leave will not be considered as non-availability. Other extenuating circumstances, as determined by the SQ/CC, that prevent the crewmember from mission duties for more than 15 consecutive days may be considered as non-availability for proration purposes. The following guidelines apply:

4.10.1.1. Proration will not be used to mask training or planning deficiencies.

4.10.1.2. Proration is based on cumulative days of non-availability for mission duties in the training cycle. Use Table 4.2 to determine the number of months to be prorated based on each period of cumulative non-mission duty calendar days. **(T-3)**

4.10.1.3. If MQT is re-accomplished, a crewmember's training cycle will start over at a prorated share following completion of MQT. **(T-3)**

4.10.1.4. No requirement may be prorated below one. Prorated numbers resulting in fractions of less than 0.5 will be rounded to the next lower whole number (one or greater). **(T-3)**

4.10.1.5. Newly assigned crewmembers achieving MR or BMC status after the 15th of the month are considered to be in CT on the first day of the following month for proration purposes. A prorated share of RCP missions must be completed in CT. **(T-3)**

4.10.1.6. A crewmember's last month on station prior to PCSing may be prorated provided 1 month's proration is not exceeded. Individuals PCSing may be considered MR for reporting purposes during a period of 60 days from date of last mission/sortie, or until loss of MR currency, port call date, or sign in at new duty station, whichever occurs first. **(T-3)**

4.10.1.7. Activated ARC members on orders for 30 consecutive days or greater, will maintain active duty proficiencies and currency requirements prorated for the duration they are on orders. **(T-3)**

**4.11. Operational Missions.** The following procedures are intended to provide flexibility in accomplishing the unit's CT program. Sorties conducted during operational missions will be logged. These sorties count toward annual RCP requirements and will be used for lookback purposes. Operational missions and events may be used to update proficiency/currency requirements if they meet the criteria in Attachment 2. **(T-3)**

4.11.1. Example: Capt Jones was granted 17 days of emergency leave in January and attended SOS in residence from March through April for 56 consecutive calendar days. The SQ/CC authorized a total of two months proration from his training cycle (two months for the 73 cumulative days of non-availability).

**Table 4.2. Proration Allowance. (T-3).**

| CUMULATIVE DAYS OF NON-MISSION ACTIVITY | PRORATION ALLOWED (Months) |
|---|---|
| 0 – 15 | 0 |
| 16 – 45 | 1 |
| 46 – 75 | 2 |
| 76 – 105 | 3 |
| 106 – 135 | 4 |
| 136 – 165 | 5 |
| 166 – 195 | 6 |
| 196 – 225 | 7 |
| 226 – 255 | 8 |
| 256 – 285 | 9 |
| 286 – 315 | 10 |
| 316 – 345 | 11 |
| Over 345 | 12 |

**4.12. Regaining MR or BMC Status.**

4.12.1. If MR or BMC status is lost due to failure to meet the end of cycle event requirements, re-certification/re-qualification is IAW paragraph 4.10. **(T-3)**

4.12.2. If MR or BMC status is lost due to failure to meet lookback IAW paragraph 4.10, the following applies (timing starts from the date the crewmember came off MR or BMC status): **(T-3)**

4.12.2.1. Up to 90 Days. Complete a SQ/CC approved recertification program (documented in the individual's training folder) to return the crewmember to MR or BMC standards. Upon completion of the recertification program, the MR or BMC crewmember must also meet the subsequent 1-month lookback requirement prior to reclaiming MR or BMC status. The missions and events accomplished during the recertification program may be credited towards their total/type mission and event requirements for the training cycle as well as for their monthly mission requirement. In addition, all RCP event currencies must be regained. The SQ/CC will approve any other additional training prior to MR recertification. **(T-3)**

4.12.2.2. 91-180 Days. Same as above, plus open/closed book qualification examinations (IAW AFI 17-202V2. Open/closed book exams will be documented IAW AFI 17-202V2. **(T-3)**

4.12.2.3. 181 Days and Beyond. Reaccomplish a SQ/CC-directed MQT program to include a formal MSN evaluation IAW AFI 17-202V2, applicable HHQ guidance, and AFI 17-2AFINCV2. **(T-3)**

**Figure 4.1.  Regression Flow Chart.**

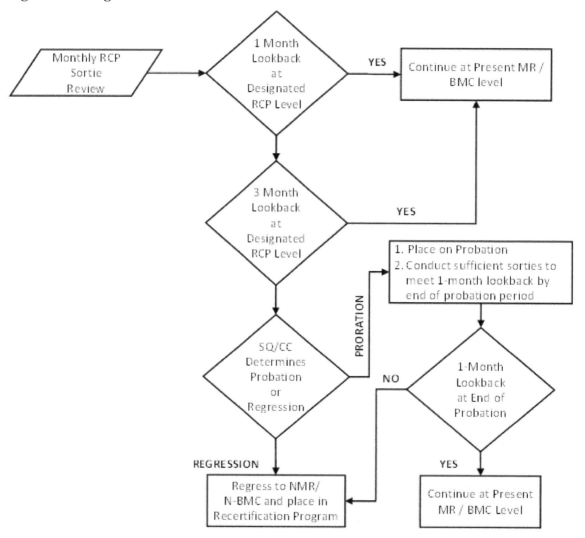

**Chapter 5**

**UPGRADE AND SPECIALIZED MISSION TRAINING**

**5.1. General.** This chapter outlines duties and responsibilities for units to upgrade, certify, and maintain currency/proficiency for special capabilities, and certifications/qualifications. SQ/CCs may tailor programs for individuals based on previous experience, qualifications, and documented performance. These capabilities and certifications/qualifications are in addition to unit core missions and do not apply to every crewmember assigned or attached to the unit. **(T-3)**

**5.2. Requirements.** Requirements for upgrade and special mission training are listed in Table 1.1. Additionally, commanders must ensure each candidate has the ability, judgment, technical expertise, skill, and experience when selecting a crewmember for upgrade or specialized mission training. Prerequisites can be waived by SQ/CC. **(T-3)**

**5.3. Instructor Upgrade.** This section establishes the minimum guidelines for instructor upgrade.

5.3.1. Instructor Responsibilities. An AF instructor shall be a competent subject matter expert adept in the methodology of instruction. The instructor shall be proficient in evaluating, diagnosing, and critiquing student performance, identifying learning objectives and difficulties, and prescribing and conducting remedial instruction. The instructor must be able to conduct instruction in all training venues (e.g., classroom, training devices, ops floor, mission execution, etc.) **(T-3)**

5.3.1.1. Instructor Prerequisites. SQ/CCs will consider ability, judgment, technical expertise, skill, and experience when selecting a crewmember for instructor upgrade. **(T-3)**

5.3.1.2. For instructor minimum requirements, see Table 1.1, section 1.6. All instructor candidates will be MR in their unit's mission. USAF Weapons School (USAFWS) graduates are instructor qualified. **(T-3)**

5.3.1.3. Training. Instructor training will include methodology of instruction, Air Force tasking process, mission planning, and unit mission employment at the minimum (e.g., tasked mission types). The instructor candidate must be able to conduct instruction in all training venues (e.g., classroom, training devices, ops floor, mission execution, etc.). **(T-3)**

5.3.1.4. Mission Execution. Instructors teaching this course may receive credit to update their instructor currency. **(T-3)**

5.3.1.5. Testing. Units will develop tests based on the training requirements in AFI 17-202V1, HHQ supplements, this publication, and other relevant guidance. Test will be closed book and consist of a minimum of 25 questions. To received credit for this training each instructor candidate must pass the test with a minimum score of 80 percent. Units will develop and maintain an instructor test master question file. **(T-3)**

5.3.1.6. Qualification and Certification. All instructor candidates will demonstrate to an evaluator their ability to instruct and perform selected tasks and items according to applicable directives. Following successful completion of instructor training and evaluation, the SQ/CC or designated representative will personally interview the candidate and review instructor responsibilities, scope of duties, authority, and philosophy. SQ/CC will certify a new instructor by placing a letter of certification in the training folder and indicate qualifications on a letter of Xs. **(T-3)**

WILLIAM J. BENDER, Lt Gen, USAF
Chief of Information Dominance and
Chief Information Officer

## Attachment 1

## GLOSSARY OF REFERENCES AND SUPPORTING INFORMATION

*References*

Privacy Act (5 U.S.C. § 552a)

AFPD 17-2, *Cyberspace Operations,* 12 April 2016

AFI 17-202 Volume 1, *Cybercrew Training,* 2 Apr 2014

AFI 17-202 Volume 2, *Cybercrew Standardization and Evaluation Program,* 15 October 2014

AFI 17-2AFINCV2, *Air Force Intranet Control (AFNIC) Standardization and Evaluation*

AFI 17-2 AFNICV3, *Air Force Intranet Network Control (AFNIC) Operations and Procedures*

AFI 33-360, *Publications and Forms Management,* 1 December 2015

AFMAN 33-363, *Management of Records,* 1 March 2008, (*Incorporating Change* 2, 9 June 2016, *Certified Current* 21 July 2016).

AFPAM 90-803, *Risk Management (RM) Guidelines and Tools*, 11 February 2013

*Adopted Forms*

AF Form 847, *Recommendation for Change of Publication*

*Abbreviations and Acronyms*

**AF**—Air Force

**AFI**—Air Force Instruction

**AFINC**—Air Force Intranet Control

**AFMAN**—Air Force Manual

**AFPD**—Air Force Policy Document

**AFRC**—Air Force Reserve Command

**AFRIMS**—Air Force Records Information Management System

**AFSPC**—Air Force Space Command

**AFTTP**—Air Force Tactics, Techniques and Procedures

**ANG**—Air National Guard

**ARC**—Air Reserve Components

**BCQ**—Basic Cyber Qualified

**BMC**—Basic Mission Capable

**C2**—Command & Control

**CC**—Commander

**CD**—Deputy Commander

**CFT**—Composite Force Training

**CMR**—Combat Mission Ready

**CPI**—Cybercrew Position Indicator

**CT**—Continuation Training

**CV**—Vice Commander

**CW**—Cyberspace Wing

**DCC – Defensive Counter**—Cyber

**DCO**—Defensive cyber operations

**DO**—Director of Operations

**DOC**—Designed Operational Capability

**DOK**—Weapons and Tactics Office

**DOT**—Unit Training Office

**EXP**— Experienced

**FLT**—Flight

**FTU**—Formal Training Unit

**HQ**—Headquarters

**HHQ**—Higher Headquarters

**IAW**—In Accordance With

**INEXP**—Inexperienced

**IP**—Internet Protocol

**IQT**—Initial Qualification Training

**JFT**—Joint Force Training

**LFE**—Large Force Exercise

**LIMFAC**—Limiting Factor

**MAJCOM**—Major Command

**MC**—Mission Commander

**MQT**—Mission Qualification Training

**MR**—Mission Ready

**N-BMC –** Non-Basic Mission Capable

**NGB**—National Guard Bureau

**NMR –** Non-Mission Ready

**OG**—Operations Group

**OPORD**—Operations Order

**OPR**—Office of Primary Responsibility

**OSS**—Operations Support Squadron

**PBED**—Planning, Briefing, Execution, and Debriefing

**PCS**—Permanent Change of Station

**QRF**—Quick Reaction Force

**RCD**—Records Disposition Schedule

**RCP**—Ready Cybercrew Program

**ROC**—Rehearsal of Concept

**ROE**—Rules of Engagement

**RT**—Requalification training

**RTM**—Ready Tasking Memorandum

**RTRB**—Realistic Training Review Board

**SORTS**—Status of Resources and Training

**SQ**—Squadron

**Stan/Evals**—Standardization and evaluation

**TDY**—Temporary Duty

**TTP**—Tactics, Tips and Procedures

**TRP**—Tactical Reconnaissance Package

**USAF**—United States Air Force

**USAFWS**—United States Air Force Weapons School

**WG**— Wing

**WIC**—Weapons Instructor Course

*Terms*

**Additional Training**—Any training recommended to remedy deficiencies identified during an evaluation that must be completed by a specific due date. This training may include self-study, CTD, or simulator. Additional training must include demonstration of satisfactory knowledge or proficiency to examiner, supervisor or instructor (as stipulated in the Additional Training description) to qualify as completed.

**Attached Personnel**—This includes anyone not assigned to the unit but maintaining qualification through that unit. AFRC, ANG, and HAF augmented personnel are an example of attached personnel.

**Basic Cyber Qualified (BCQ)**—A crewmember member who satisfactorily completed IQT. The crewmember is BCQ only until completion of MQT. BCQ crewmembers will only perform RCP-tasked events or sorties under instructor supervision.

**Basic Mission Capable (BMC)**—A crewmember member who satisfactorily completed IQT and MQT, but is not in fully-certified MR status. A BMC crewmember accomplishes the training required to remain familiarized in all and may be qualified and proficient in some of the primary missions of their weapon system BMC requirements. These crewmembers may also maintain special mission qualification.

**Certification**—Designation of an individual by the certifying official (normally the SQ/CC) as having completed required training and being capable of performing a specific duty.

**Continuation Training (CT)**— Training which provides crew members with the volume, frequency, and mix of training necessary to maintain currency and proficiency in the assigned qualification level.

**Currency**—A measure of how frequently and/or recently a task is completed. Currency requirements should ensure the average crewmember member maintains a minimum level of proficiency in a given event.

**Cybercrew Position Indicator (CPI)**—Codes used to manage crewmember positions to ensure a high state of readiness is maintained with available resources.

**Cyberspace Operations (CO)**—The employment of cyberspace capabilities where the primary purpose is to achieve objectives in or through cyberspace.

**Experienced Crewmember (EXP)**—Management term describing crewmember who meet the requirement as dictated within the weapon system specific volumes.

**Initial Qualification Training (IQT)**—Weapon system-specific training designed to cover system specific and/or positional specific training leading to declaration of BCQ as a prerequisite to Mission Qualification Training (MQT).

**Instructor**—An experienced individual qualified to instruct other individuals in mission area academics and positional duties. Instructors will be qualified appropriately to the level of the training they provide.

**Instructor Event**—An event logged by an instructor when performing instructor duties during the sortie, or a portion thereof. Instructor qualification required and used for the mission or a mission element. Examples include upgrade sorties, updating lost currencies, etc. Instructors will log this event on evaluation sorties.

**Mission**—A set of tasks that lead to an objective, to include associated planning, brief, execution, and debrief.

**Mission Qualification Training (MQT)**—Following IQT, MQT is a formal training program used to qualify crewmember members in assigned crew positions to perform the unit mission. This training is required to achieve a basic level of competence in unit's primary tasked missions and is a prerequisite for MR or BMC declaration.

**Mission Ready (MR)**—The status of a crewmember member who has satisfactorily completed IQT, MQT, and maintains certification, currency and proficiency in the command or unit operational mission.

**Proficiency**—A measure of how well a task is completed. A crewmember member is considered proficient when they can perform tasks at the minimum acceptable levels of speed, accuracy, and safety.

**Qualification (QUAL)**—Designation of an individual by the unit commander as having completed required training and evaluation and being capable of performing a specific duty.

**Ready Cybercrew Program (RCP)**—Annual sortie/event training requirements for crewmembers to maintain mission ready/combat mission ready (MR) status.

**Sortie**—The actions an individual cyberspace weapon system takes to accomplish a mission and/or mission objective(s) within a defined start and stop period.

**Specialized Mission Training**—Training in any special skills (e.g., tactics, weapon system capabilities, responsibilities, etc.) necessary to carry out the unit's assigned missions that are not required by every crew member. Specialized training is normally accomplished after the crew member is assigned MR or BMC status, and is normally in addition to MR or BMC requirements. This training may require an additional certification and/or qualification event as determined by the SQ/CC.

**Squadron Supervisor**—May include all or some of the following depending on specific guidance and SQ/CC concurrence: SQ/CC, SQ/DO, ADOs, and FLT/CCs.

**Supervisory Crewmember or Staff Member**—Personnel in supervisory or staff positions (CPI-6/8/B/D) who actively conduct cyber operations.

**Supervised Status**—The status of a crew member who must perform mission under the supervision of an instructor.

**Training Level**—Assigned to individuals based on the continuation training status (basic cyber qualification, basic mission capable, or mission ready/combat mission ready) they are required to maintain.

**Training Period**—Any training period determined by the wing in which training requirements are performed.

**Upgrade Training**—Training needed to qualify to a crew position of additional responsibility for a specific weapon system (e.g., special mission qualifications). See special mission event training.

**Attachment 2**

**GLOSSARY OF MISSION, SORTIE AND EVENT DEFINITIONS**

**A2.1. Mission and Sortie Definitions:**

A2.1.1. See 624th Operations Center portal for latest information.

**A2.2. Mission, Sortie and Event Identifiers and Descriptions:**

A2.2.1. Mission-Related Training. Mission-related training is training required of all crewmembers as part of their CT program. Where conflict exists between this guidance and the RTM, the RTM takes precedence.

A2.2.1.1. GTR001 Weapons and Tactics Training.

A2.2.1.1.1. Purpose: To provide the crewmember with the information necessary for effective and successful execution of the unit's assigned mission.

A2.2.1.1.2. Description: GTR001 will be administered using courseware developed by the unit. The course will be based on information found in AFTTP 3-1, AFTTP 3-3, AFI 17-2AFINCV3 as well as other documents relevant to the execution of the unit's mission.

A2.2.1.1.3. OPR: Unit/Weapons and Tactics Office (DOK)

A2.2.1.1.4. Course Developer: Unit/DOK

A2.2.1.1.5. Training Media: Lecture

A2.2.1.1.6. Instructor Requirements: Academic instructors should be WIC graduates or have attended the applicable academic portion(s) of school, if possible.

A2.2.1.1.7. Additional Information: Instructors teaching GTR001 may receive credit for their GTR001 requirement.

A2.2.1.2. GTR002 Crew Risk Management (CRM) Training.

A2.2.1.2.1. Purpose: To provide crewmembers with unit CRM training according to AF Pamphlet 90-803 and other RM resources, and MAJCOM Supplements.

A2.2.1.2.2. Description: GTR002 will be administered using unit developed courseware. CRM training introduces the common core CRM subjects to provide crewmembers with the information necessary to enhance mission effectiveness. Training should create a cultural mindset in which every crewmember is trained and motivated to manage risk and integrates CRM into mission and activity planning process ensuring decisions are based upon risk assessment of the operation/activity. CRM training will be tailored to meet the unique mission needs and operational requirements of each organization and to the personnel within the organization.

A2.2.1.2.3. OPR: Unit

A2.2.1.2.4. Course Developer: Unit

A2.2.1.2.5. Training Media: Lecture

A2.2.1.2.6.  Additional Information:  CRM instructors teaching GTR002 may receive credit for their GTR002 requirement.

**A2.3.  AFINC Events**

A2.3.1.  EV001 Distributed Denial of Service (DDOS)

A2.3.1.1.  Purpose:  Detect and defeat a DDOS attack

A2.3.1.1.1.  Description:  A coordinated effort to employ the weapon system to counter an attack that uses a number of hosts to overwhelm devices on a network or enclave, causing a host to experience a complete system crash.

A2.3.1.1.2.  OPR: Unit/DOT

A2.3.1.1.3.  Course Developer: Unit/DOT

A2.3.1.1.4.  Training Media:  Weapon system or simulator

A2.3.1.1.5.  Instructor Requirements: Certified AFINC Instructor

A2.3.1.1.6.  Additional Information:  Student assessment via instructor observation

A2.3.1.2.  EV002 Malicious Email

A2.3.1.2.1.  Purpose:  Detect and defeat a malicious email

A2.3.1.2.2.  Description: A coordinated effort to employ the weapon system to counter nefarious email which may contain malicious logic and/or malicious URLs.

A2.3.1.2.3.  OPR: Unit/DOT

A2.3.1.2.4.  Course Developer: Unit/DOT

A2.3.1.2.5.  Training Media:  Weapon system or simulator

A2.3.1.2.6.  Instructor Requirements: Certified AFINC Instructor

A2.3.1.2.7.  Additional Information: Student assessment via instructor observation

A2.3.1.3.  EV003 Data Exfiltration Attempt

A2.3.1.3.1.  Purpose: Detect and defeat a Data Exfiltration Attempt

A2.3.1.3.2.  Description: A coordinated effort to employ the weapon system to counter the adversary conducting data exfiltration from the AFIN.

A2.3.1.3.3.  OPR: Unit/DOT

A2.3.1.3.4.  Course Developer: Unit/DOT

A2.3.1.3.5.  Training Media:  Weapon system or simulator

A2.3.1.3.6.  Instructor Requirements: Certified AFINC Instructor

A2.3.1.3.7.  Additional Information: Student assessment via instructor observation

A2.3.1.4.  EV004 Rogue Network Devices

A2.3.1.4.1.  Purpose: Detect and remove a rogue network device

A2.3.1.4.2. Description: A coordinated effort to employ the weapon system to counter and remove a rogue network device from the AFINC.

A2.3.1.4.3. OPR: Unit/DOT

A2.3.1.4.4. Course Developer: Unit/DOT

A2.3.1.4.5. Training Media:  Weapon system or simulator

A2.3.1.4.6. Instructor Requirements: Certified AFINC Instructor

A2.3.1.4.7. Additional Information: Student assessment via instructor observation

A2.3.1.5.  EV005 AFIN Malware Propagation

A2.3.1.5.1. Purpose: Detect and isolate propagating malware

A2.3.1.5.2. Description: A coordinated effort to employ the weapon system to counter and/or isolate malicious logic propagating on the AFIN.

A2.3.1.5.3. OPR: Unit/DOT

A2.3.1.5.4. Course Developer: Unit/DOT

A2.3.1.5.5. Training Media:  Weapon system or simulator

A2.3.1.5.6. Instructor Requirements: Certified AFINC Instructor

A2.3.1.5.7. Additional Information: Student assessment via instructor observation

A2.3.1.6.  EV006 Enclave to Enclave Exploitation

A2.3.1.6.1. Purpose: Detect, isolate and/or mitigate inter enclave exploitation

A2.3.1.6.2. Description: A coordinated effort to employ the weapon system to counter or isolate inter enclave exploitation on the AFIN.

A2.3.1.6.3. OPR: Unit/DOT

A2.3.1.6.4. Course Developer: Unit/DOT

A2.3.1.6.5. Training Media:  Weapon system or simulator

A2.3.1.6.6. Instructor Requirements: Certified AFINC Instructor

A2.3.1.6.7. Additional Information: Student assessment via instructor observation

A2.3.1.7.  EV007 Host to Host Exploitation

A2.3.1.7.1. Purpose: Detect and defeat AFIN host compromise

A2.3.1.7.2. Description: A coordinated effort to employ the weapon system to counter inter host exploitation on the AFIN.

A2.3.1.7.3. OPR: Unit/DOT

A2.3.1.7.4. Course Developer: Unit/DOT

A2.3.1.7.5. Training Media:  Weapon system or simulator

A2.3.1.7.6. Instructor Requirements: Certified AFINC Instructor

A2.3.1.7.7. Additional Information: Student assessment via instructor observation

A2.3.1.8.  EV008 C2 Channel ID

A2.3.1.8.1.  Purpose: Detect and defeat an adversary C2 channel on the AFIN

A2.3.1.8.2.  Description: A coordinated effort to employ the weapon system to counter an adversary C2 channel on the AFIN.

A2.3.1.8.3.  OPR: Unit/DOT

A2.3.1.8.4.  Course Developer: Unit/DOT

A2.3.1.8.5.  Training Media:  Weapon system or simulator

A2.3.1.8.6.  Instructor Requirements: Certified AFINC Instructor

A2.3.1.8.7.  Additional Information: Student assessment via instructor observation

A2.3.1.9.  EV009 Weapon System Component Compromise

A2.3.1.9.1.  Purpose: Detect and respond to Weapon System compromise

A2.3.1.9.2.  Description: Identify and counter threats to components of the AFINC Weapon System.

A2.3.1.9.3.  OPR: Unit/DOT

A2.3.1.9.4.  Course Developer: Unit/DOT

A2.3.1.9.5.  Training Media:  Weapon system or simulator

A2.3.1.9.6.  Instructor Requirements: Certified AFINC Instructor

A2.3.1.9.7.  Additional Information: Student assessment via instructor observation

A2.3.2. Unit Defined ("XTR") Training Requirements. XTR is reserved for use by local units. Publish OG/CC level guidance documenting local event identifiers, associated nomenclature, volume, currency and frequency. OG/CC should review all "XTR" training requirements for relevancy to the unit's mission.

**Attachment 3**

**WHITE CARD SCENARIOS**

**A3.1.  White-Card scenarios:**

A3.1.1. Initiating the White-card Scenario:   When you use white-card scenario's, the instructor/evaluator will brief the member on the nature of the scenario, highlighting which actions should be simulated and which should be acted out. Once the member verifies understanding, the instructor/evaluator will hand the member the scenario's *Task Card* while retaining the *Training Scenario – XXX (Instructor Card)*.

A3.1.2. Administering the Scenario:   The instructor/evaluator will observe the member's execution of the task listed on the *Task Card*. The instructor/evaluator should look for the member to perform actions listed on the *Instructor Card* and make note of completion or omission (note:  all actions might not be taken in the sequence listed on the *Instructor Card*).

**Attachment 4**

**CYBERCREW RESOURCE MANAGEMENT**

**A4.1. Crewmember inventory requires** close management at all levels to ensure a high state of readiness is maintained with available resources. To manage crewmember inventory, Cybercrew Position Indicator (CPI) codes are assigned to identify these positions.

**Table A4.1. Cybercrew Position Indicator (CPI) Codes.**

| CPI Codes | Explanation | Remarks |
|---|---|---|
| 1 | Crewmember position used primarily for weapon system operations (Officer). | See Note 1 |
| 2 | Crewmember position used primarily for weapon system operations (Government Civilians). | See Note 1 |
| 3 | Staff or supervisory positions at wing level and below that have responsibilities and duties that require cyberspace operations expertise but which do not require the incumbents to operate the weapon system. | See Note 2 |
| 4 | Staff or supervisory positions above the wing level that have responsibilities and duties that require cyberspace operations expertise but which do not require the incumbents to operate the weapon system. | See Note 2 |
| 6 | Staff or supervisory positions at wing level and below that have responsibilities and duties that require the incumbents to actively perform cyberspace operational duties on the weapon system. | See Note 2 |
| 8 | Staff or supervisory positions above the wing level that have responsibilities and duties that require the incumbent to actively conduct cyberspace operations on the weapon system. | See Note 2 |
| A | Crew positions used for primarily for weapon system operations (Enlisted). | See Note 1 |
| B | Staff or supervisory positions at wing level and below that have responsibilities and duties that require the incumbents to actively perform cyberspace operational duties on the weapon system. | See Note 2 |
| C | Staff or supervisory positions at wing level and below that have responsibilities and duties that require cyberspace operations expertise but which do not require the incumbents to actively operate the weapon system. | See Note 2 |
| D | Staff or supervisory positions above the wing level that have responsibilities and duties that require the incumbent to actively conduct cyberspace operations on a weapon system. | See Note 2 |
| E | Staff or supervisory positions above the wing level that have responsibilities and duties that require cyberspace operations expertise but which do not require the incumbents to actively operate the weapon system. | See Note 2 |
| Z | Crewmember positions used primarily for weapon system operations (Contractor). | See Note 1 |

*Notes:*

1. CPI-1, 2, A and Z are for officers, enlisted, government civilian, and contractor personnel assigned to operational squadrons or formal training programs. The primary duty of these personnel is to operate the weapon system to conduct cyberspace operations.

2. CPI-3, 4, 6, 8, B, C, D, and E identify crewmember members assigned to supervisory or staff positions. These positions require cyberspace operations experience with some requiring weapon system operation (CPI-6, 8, B, and D).

BY ORDER OF THE SECRETARY
OF THE AIR FORCE

AIR FORCE INSTRUCTION 17-2AFINC
VOLUME 2

23 MAY 2017

Cyberspace

AIR FORCE INTRANET CONTROL
(AFINC) STANDARDIZATION
AND EVALUATION

## COMPLIANCE WITH THIS PUBLICATION IS MANDATORY

**ACCESSIBILITY:** Publications and forms are available for downloading or ordering on the e- Publishing website at www.e-Publishing.af.mil

**RELEASABILITY:** There are no releasability restrictions on this publication

OPR: A3CX/A6CX

Certified by: AF/A3C/A6C
(Col Donald J. Fielden)
Pages: 29

This Instruction implements Air Force (AF) Policy Directive (AFPD) 17-2, *Cyberspace Operations* and references Air Force Instruction (AFI) 17-202V2, *Cybercrew Standardization and Evaluation Program*. It establishes the Crew Standardization and Evaluation (Stan/Eval) procedures and evaluation criteria for qualifying crew members in the Air Force Intranet Network Control (AFINC) weapon system. This publication applies to all military and civilian AF personnel, members of AF Reserve Command (AFRC) units and the Air National Guard (ANG). Refer to paragraph 1.3 for information on the authority to waive provisions of this AFI. This publication may be supplemented at the unit level, but all direct supplements must be routed through channels to HQ USAF/A3C/A6C for coordination prior to certification and approval. The authorities to waive wing/unit level requirements in this publication are identified with a Tier ("T-0, T-1, T-2, T-3") number following the compliance statement. See AFI 33-360, *Publications and Forms Management*, Table 1.1 for a description of the authorities associated with the Tier numbers. Submit requests for waivers through the chain of command to the appropriate Tier waiver approval authority, or alternately, to the Publication OPR for non-tiered compliance items. Send recommended changes or comments to the Office of Primary Responsibility (OPR) (HQ USAF/A3C/A6C, 1480 Air Force Pentagon, Washington, DC 20330-1480), using AF Form 847, *Recommendation for Change of Publication*; route AF Forms 847 from the field through the chain of command. This Instruction requires collecting and maintaining information protected by the Privacy Act of 1974 (5 U.S.C. 552a). System of records notices F036 AF PC C, Military Personnel Records System, and OPM/GOVT-1, General Personnel Records, apply. When collecting and maintaining information protect it by the Privacy

Act of 1974 authorized by 10 U.S.C. 8013. Ensure that all records created as a result of processes prescribed in this publication are maintained IAW Air Force Manual (AFMAN) 33-363, *Management of Records*, and disposed of IAW the Air Force Records Disposition Schedule (RDS) in the Air Force Records Information Management System (AFRIMS).

This volume contains references to the following field (subordinate level) publications and forms which, until converted to departmental level publications and forms may be obtained from the respective MAJCOM publication office:

**Chapter 1— GENERAL INFORMATION**     **4**

    1.1.    General................................................................................... 4

    1.2.    Recommendation for Change of Publication ............................................ 4

    1.3.    Waivers ................................................................................... 4

    1.4.    Procedures:............................................................................... 4

    1.5.    General Evaluation Requirements: ..................................................... 5

Table    1.1.    Crew Position/SMQ Specific Requirements - Written Examinations. ............... 7

    1.6.    Grading Instructions ..................................................................... 8

Table    1.2.    Crew Position/SMQ Specific Requirements - Performance Phase Evaluations..... 9

**Chapter 2— CREW POSITION EVALUATIONS AND GRADING CRITERIA**     **10**

    2.1.    General................................................................................... 10

    2.2.    Qualification Evaluations: .............................................................. 10

    2.3.    Mission Certifications................................................................... 10

    2.4.    General Crew Position Evaluation Criteria............................................ 10

    2.5.    AFINC Operator SMQ Evaluation Criteria. ......................................... 16

**Chapter 3— INSTRUCTOR EVALUATIONS AND GRADING CRITERIA**     **18**

    3.1.    General................................................................................... 18

    3.2.    Instructor Upgrade and Qualification Requisites..................................... 18

    3.3.    Instructor Qualification Evaluations .................................................. 18

    3.4.    Instructor Evaluation Grading Criteria ............................................... 18

    3.5.    Instructor Evaluation Documentation ................................................. 20

**Chapter 4— SEE OBJECTIVITY EVALUATIONS AND GRADING CRITERIA**                **22**

    4.1.    General........................................................................................................  22

    4.2.    Evaluator Upgrade and Qualification Requisites.......................................  22

    4.3.    SEE Objectivity Evaluations.....................................................................  22

    4.4.    SEE Objectivity Evaluation Grading Criteria...........................................  23

    4.5.    SEE Objectivity Evaluation Documentation..............................................  25

**Attachment 1— GLOSSARY OF REFERENCES AND SUPPORTING INFORMATION**                **26**

**Chapter 1**

**GENERAL INFORMATION**

**1.1. General** . This instruction provides cyberspace operations examiners and cybercrew members with procedures and evaluation criteria used during performance evaluations on the Air Force Intranet Control weapon system. Adherence to these procedures and criteria will ensure an accurate assessment of the proficiency and capabilities of cyber crewmembers. In addition to general criteria information and grading criteria, this AFI provides specific information and grading criteria for each crew position, special mission qualification (SMQ), instructor upgrade qualification, and Stan/Eval examiner objectivity evaluations.

**1.2. Recommendation for Change of Publication** . Recommendations for changes to this volume will be submitted on AF Form 847, through the appropriate functional's chain of command to HQ USAF/A3CX/A6CX.

**1.3. Waivers** . Unless another approval authority is cited ("T-0, T-1, T-2, T-3"), waiver authority for this volume is the MAJCOM/A3 (or equivalent). Submit requests for waivers using AF Form 679, *Air Force Publication Compliance Item Waiver Request/Approval* through the chain of command to the appropriate Tier waiver approval authority. If approved, waivers remain in effect for the life of the published guidance, unless the waiver authority specifies a shorter period of time, cancels in writing, or issues a change that alters the basis for the waiver.

**1.4. Procedures:**

1.4.1. Standardization and Evaluation Examiners (SEEs) will use the grading policies contained in AFI 17-202V2 and the evaluation criteria in this instruction volume for conducting all AFSPC and AFSPC-oversight units' weapon system performance, Cybercrew Training Device (CTD), and Emergency Procedures Evaluations (EPE). All evaluations assume a stable platform and normal operating conditions. Compound emergency procedures (a scenario involving multiple emergency procedures) will not be used. **(T-2)**

1.4.2. Each squadron will design and maintain evaluation profiles for each mission/weapon system that includes information on each crew position. These profiles, approved by Operations Group Standardization/Evaluation (OGV), should outline the minimum number and type of events to be performed/observed to satisfy a complete evaluation. Evaluation profiles will incorporate requirements established in the applicable grading criteria and reflect the primary unit tasking. **(T-3)**

1.4.3. All evaluations fall under the Qualification (QUAL), Mission (MSN) or Spot (SPOT) categories in AFI 17-202V2. For dual/multiple qualification or difference evaluations that do not update an eligibility period, list as "SPOT" on the front of the AF Form 4418, *Certificate of Cybercrew Qualification*, and explain that it was a difference evaluation under "Mission Description." **(T-2)**

1.4.3.1. Schedule all evaluation activity on one mission/sortie to the greatest extent possible. All performance phase requirements should be accomplished during a training (or operational if training not available) mission/sortie. If a required event is not accomplished during a mission/sortie, Operations Group Commander (OG/CC) is the waiver authority for the event to be completed in the CTD. This may be delegated no lower than SQ/CC unless otherwise authorized in position specific chapters of this instruction volume. **(T-3)**

1.4.3.2. During all evaluations, any grading areas observed by the evaluator may be evaluated. If additional training is required for areas outside of the scheduled evaluation, document the training required under the appropriate area on the AF Form 4418.

1.4.3.3. This AFI contains a table of requirements for the written requisites and a table for the grading criteria for various evaluations. Each table may include a "Note" which refers to a general note found in the individual grading criteria, and/or a number which refers to a note shown below the table. To complete an evaluation, all areas annotated with an "R" must be successfully completed. **(T-3)**

1.4.3.4. Unit examiners may give evaluations outside of their organization to include administering evaluations between Air Force Space Command (AFSPC), AFRC and ANG provided written agreements/understandings between the affected organizations are in-place. Written agreements/understandings shall be reviewed and updated annually. **(T-3)**

1.4.3.5. Units may develop and administer supplemental evaluation criteria in addition to the required evaluation criteria in this instruction. Supplemental evaluation criteria does not supersede the evaluation criteria in this instruction and will not be administered to make the evaluation criteria of this instruction less restrictive. Supplemental evaluation criteria will be published in local supplemental guidance.

1.4.4. Momentary deviations from tolerances will not be considered in the grading, provided the examinee applies prompt corrective action and such deviations do not jeopardize safety or the mission. Cumulative deviations will be considered when determining the overall grade. The SEE will state the examinee's overall rating, review with the examinee the area grades assigned, thoroughly critique specific deviations, and recommend/assign any required additional training. **(T-2)**

1.4.5. Evaluators may be used to instruct any phase of training they are qualified to teach to capitalize on their expertise and experience. If an evaluator is an individual's primary or recommending instructor, the same evaluator shall not administer the associated evaluation. **(T-3)**

1.4.6. All crewmembers for the mission/sortie (to include students, instructors, examinees, and evaluators) will participate in and adhere to all required mission planning, mission briefing, mission execution, and mission debriefing requirements. All crewmembers must be current on the Crew Information File (CIF) and meet all Go/No-Go requirements IAW AFI 17-202 series publications, this instruction, and all applicable supplemental guidance prior to operating, instructing, or evaluating on the weapon system. **(T-2)**

**1.5. General Evaluation Requirements:**

1.5.1. Publications Check. In units where crewmembers are individually issued operating manuals, crew aids, crew aids, etc., for use in conducting operations, a publications check will be accomplished for all evaluations. The publications check will be annotated in the Comments block of the AF 4418 only if unsatisfactory. The List of Effective pages (LEP) and annual "A" page checks in individually issued operating manuals must be accomplished, documented, and current. Unit Stan/Eval will list the required operating publications each cybercrew member is responsible for in the local CIF Library and/or local supplement to AFI 17-202V2. NOTE:  In units where such resources are not individually issued but made available/accessible for common use, the squadron Stan/Eval office will list those items (version and date) and ensure the accuracy and currency of the information contained in those resources for common use. **(T- 2)**

1.5.2.  Written Examinations:

1.5.2.1.  The requisites in Table 1.1 are common to all AFINC crew positions and will be accomplished IAW AFI 17-202V2, all applicable supplemental guidance, and unit directives. These will be accomplished prior to the mission/sortie performance phase unless in conjunction with a No-notice (N/N) QUAL.  NOTE: An N/N evaluation conducted in the examinee's eligibility period and meeting all required QUAL profile requirements affords the examinee to opt for the N/N evaluation to satisfy a periodic QUAL, in which the examinee may complete written and EPE requisites after the performance phase.  However, the written examination(s) and EPE must be completed prior to the examinee's expiration date. **(T-2)**

1.5.3.  Emergency Procedures Evaluations (EPE). Every Qualification evaluation which updates an expiration date will include an EPE. Qualification EPEs will evaluate the crewmember's knowledge and/or performance of emergency procedures, to include use of emergency equipment.  Use the Emergency Procedures/Equipment grading criteria for all emergency situations given. Use Systems Knowledge/Operations grading criteria to evaluate general systems operation.  An EPE will be accomplished orally and will be conducted before, during, or after the performance phase of any applicable evaluation conducting a scenario-based evaluation using question/answer (Q&A) techniques.  Units will determine scenarios for EPEs. The SEE will assign an overall EPE grade (1 or 3).  The evaluation criteria for EPEs is defined in Area 8.  Document the accomplishment and result of the EPE in the Written Phase block of Section II Qualification on the AF Form 4418. **(T-2)**

**Table 1.1. Crew Position/SMQ Specific Requirements - Written Examinations.**

| Examination Type | CC QUAL | OC QUAL | AFINC-O QUAL | DNS/MEG | Router | Analyst |
|---|---|---|---|---|---|---|
| CLOSED BOOK (Note 1) | R | R | R | | | |
| EPE (Note 2) | R | R | R | | | |
| *SMQ CLOSED BOOK (Note 3) | | | | R | R | R |
| OPEN BOOK (Note 4) | O | O | O | O | O | O |

R – required
O – Optional

NOTES:
1. The CLOSED BOOK exam consists of 25-50 questions derived from applicable operations manuals and governing directives. **(T-2)**

2. The Emergency Procedure Examination (EPE) is required for all INIT QUAL and subsequent periodic QUAL evaluations covering duties in the member's primary crew position. **(T-2)**

3. The Special Mission Qualification (SMQ) upgrade CLOSED BOOK exam is a separate closed book exam consisting of 25-50 questions specific to the SMQ derived from applicable operations manuals and governing directives. For initial SMQ evaluations not combined with the member's periodic QUAL (for the primary crew position), the SMQ exam is the only required exam. Subsequent (periodic) SMQ evaluations should be combined with the member's periodic QUAL evaluation, therefore, requiring the written requisites to consist of the CLOSED BOOK and applicable SMQ exam(s). **(T-2)**

4. Units may opt to administer OPEN BOOK examinations to their crews to enhance operator knowledge.

1.5.4. Qualification (QUAL) Evaluations. These evaluations measure a crewmember's ability to meet grading areas listed in Table 1.2. at the end of this chapter and defined in **Chapter 2** of this instruction. IAW AFI 17-202V2 and lead MAJCOM guidance, QUAL evaluations may be combined with MSN evaluations. When practical, QUAL evaluations should be combined with Instructor evaluations, as applicable for the crew position. **(T-2)**

1.5.5. Mission (MSN) Evaluations. IAW AFI 17-202V2 and lead MAJCOM guidance, the requirement for a separate MSN evaluation may be combined with the QUAL evaluation. The various procedures and techniques used throughout the different weapon system variants are managed through a training program which results in a mission certification or culminates with a special mission qualification (SMQ). Mission certifications will be IAW AFI17-202V1, AFI 17-2AFINCV1, *Air Force Intranet Network Control (AFNIC) Training* and all applicable supplements and will be documented in the appropriate training folder.

MSN and SMQ evaluation grading areas are also listed in Table 1.2. at the end of this chapter and defined in Chapter 2 of this instruction. **(T-2)**

1.5.5.1. For cybercrew members who maintain multiple mission certifications, recurring evaluations need only evaluate the primary mission events as long as currency is maintained in all other required training events. **(T-2)**

1.5.6. Instructor Evaluations. Grading areas for these evaluations are listed in Table 1.2. at the end of this chapter. See Chapter 3 of this instruction for amplified information and grading area definitions. **(T-2)**

1.5.7. Stan/Eval Examiner (SEE) Objectivity Evaluations. Grading areas for these evaluations are listed in Table 1.2. at the end of this chapter. See Chapter 4 of this instruction for amplified information and grading area definitions. **(T-2)**

1.5.8. No-Notice Evaluations. OG/CC will determine no-notice evaluation procedures/goals. **(T-3)**

**1.6. Grading Instructions** . Standards and performance parameters are contained in AFI 17-202V2 and this instruction. Q, Q- and U ratings are used for specific evaluation areas. Q1, Q2, and Q3 are used for the overall evaluation rating. While the three-level grading system (Q, Q-, U) is used for most areas; a "Q-" grade will not be used for critical evaluation areas.

1.6.1. Critical Area/Subarea. Critical areas are events that require adequate accomplishment by the examinee to successfully and safely achieve the mission/sortie objectives and complete the evaluation. These events, if not adequately accomplished could result in mission failure, endanger human life, or cause serious injury or death. Additionally, critical areas/subareas apply to time-sensitive tasks or tasks that must be accomplished as expeditiously as possible without any intervening lower priority actions that would, in the normal sequence of events, adversely affect task performance/outcome. If an examinee receives a "U" grade in any critical area, the overall grade for the evaluation will be "Q-3." Critical areas are identified by "(C)" following the applicable area title. **(T-2)**

1.6.2. Major Area/Subarea. Major areas are events or tasks deemed integral to the performance of other tasks and required to sustain acceptable weapon system operations and mission execution. If an examinee receives a "U" grade in a non-critical area then the overall grade awarded will be no higher than "Q-2." An examinee receiving a "Q-" grade in a non-critical area or areas may still receive a "Q-1" overall grade at evaluator discretion. An overall "Q-3" can be awarded if, in the judgment of the flight examiner, there is justification based on performance in one or several areas/sub areas. Major areas are identified by "(M)" following the applicable area title. **(T-2)**

1.6.3. Minor Area/Subarea. Minor areas are rudimentary or simple tasks related to weapons system operations that by themselves have little or no impact on mission execution. Minor areas are identified by "(m)" following the applicable area title.

1.6.4. If an examinee receives a "U" grade in a non-critical (major or minor) area then the overall grade awarded will be no higher than "Q-2." An examinee receiving a "Q-" grade in a non-critical area or areas may still receive a "Q-1" overall grade at evaluator discretion. An overall "Q-3" can be awarded if, in the judgment of the SEE, there is justification based on performance in one or several areas/sub areas. **(T-2)**

1.6.5. The SEE must exercise judgment when the wording of areas is subjective and when specific situations are not covered.

1.6.6. Evaluator judgment will be the final determining factor in deciding the overall qualification level.

**Table 1.2.  Crew Position/SMQ Specific Requirements - Performance Phase Evaluations.**

| AREA/TITLE | Category | Crew Position | | | Special Msn Qual | | | Upgrade | |
|---|---|---|---|---|---|---|---|---|---|
| | C, M | CC | OC | O | DNS/ MEG | RTR | BP | INSTR | SEE |
| 1.  Mission Planning | M | R | R | R | | | | | |
| 2.  Systems / Equipment Knowledge | M | R | R | R | | | | | |
| 3.  Briefing | M | R | R | R | | | | | |
| 4.  Positional Changeover Brief | M, Note 1 | R | R | R | | | | | |
| 5.  Pre-Sortie Check Procedures | M | R | R | R | | | | | |
| 6.  Situational Awareness | C | R | R | R | | | | | |
| 7.  Safety | C | R | R | R | | | | | |
| 8.  Emergency Equipment / Procedures | M | R | R | R | | | | | |
| 9.  Crew Discipline | C | R | R | R | | | | | |
| 10.  Crew Coordination | M | R | R | R | | | | | |
| 11.  Communication | M | R | R | R | | | | | |
| 12.  Task Management | M | R | R | R | | | | | |
| 13.  Reports, Logs and Forms | M | R | R | R | | | | | |
| 14.  Crew Debrief | M | R | R | R | | | | | |
| 15.  Composite Force/Mutual Support | M | R | R | | | | | | |
| 16.  Cyberspace Collection | M | | | R | | | | | |
| 17.  Cyberspace Strike | M, 2 | | | | R, 3 | R, 3 | R, 3 | | |
| 18.  Cyberspace Control | M, 2 | | | | R, 3 | R, 3 | R, 3 | | |
| 19.  Weapon System Threat Correlation/Analysis | M, 2 | | | | | | | | |
| **Instructor Grading Criteria** | | | | | | | | | |
| 20.  Instructional Ability | M | | | | | | | R | |
| 21.  Instructional Briefings/Critique | M | | | | | | | R | |
| 22.  Demonstration and Performance | M | | | | | | | R | |
| **Stan/Eval Examiner Objectivity Evaluation Criteria** | | | | | | | | | |
| 23.  Compliance with Directives | M | | | | | | | | R |
| 24.  SEE Briefing | M | | | | | | | | R |
| 25.  Performance Assessment /Grading | M | | | | | | | | R |
| 26.  Additional Training Assignment | M | | | | | | | | R |
| 27.  Examinee Debrief | M | | | | | | | | R |
| 28.  Supervisor Debrief | M | | | | | | | | R |
| 29.  SEE Performance/Documentation | M | | | | | | | | R |

C – critical; M – major; R – required

NOTES:

1. Applicable for shift/crew changeovers.

2. SMQ grading areas are additional grading areas. Areas 2 – 11 and 13 – 16 also apply for SMQ periodic evaluations.

3.  Grading areas 17-19 only apply to those AFINC-O crewmembers with a SMQ that are selectively designated and qualified to perform additional strike, assurance and/or analyst duties.

**Chapter 2**

**CREW POSITION EVALUATIONS AND GRADING CRITERIA**

**2.1. General.** The grading criteria contained in this chapter are applicable to evaluations for AFINC Crew Commanders (CC), Operations Controllers (OC) and AFINC Operators (AFINC-O), and were established by experience, policies, and procedures set forth in weapon system manuals and other directives. Evaluators must realize that grading criteria contained herein cannot accommodate every situation. Written parameters must be tempered with mission objectives and, more importantly, mission/task accomplishment in the determination of overall aircrew performance. **(T-3)** Requirements for each evaluation are as follows:

**2.2. Qualification Evaluations:**

2.2.1. Written Examination Requisites: See Table 1.1 **(T-3)**

2.2.2. Emergency Procedures Evaluations: See paragraph 1.5.3.

2.2.3. Performance Phase: Required Areas 1 through 19 in Table 1.2 under CC, OC, or, AFINC-O, or AFINC-O Areas 19 to 22 will be evaluated, unless not applicable as noted. **(T-3)**

**2.3. Mission Certifications** . Mission Certifications ensure individuals are capable of performing duties essential to the effective employment of the weapon system. Mission Certifications are accomplished IAW local training requirements and/or Squadron Commander (SQ/CC) directions. Mission certification events are normally performed during Qualification evaluations, but may be performed on any mission/sortie with an instructor certified in that mission. **(T-3)**

**2.4. General Crew Position Evaluation Criteria** . The following general evaluation grading criteria are common to all crew positions unless indicated, regardless of special mission qualification(s) and additional certifications, and will be used for all applicable evaluations: **(T-3)**

2.4.1. AREA 1, Mission Planning (M)

2.4.1.1. Q. Led or contributed to mission planning efforts IAW procedures prescribed in applicable guidance manuals, instructions, and/or directives. Planning adequately addressed mission objectives and/or tasking. Plan adequately considered intelligence information, weapon system capability/operating status, and crew composition/ability with minor errors/deviations/omissions that did not impact mission effectiveness. **(T-3)**

2.4.1.2. Q-. Errors/deviations/omissions had minor impact on mission effectiveness or efficiencies, but did not impact mission accomplishment or jeopardize mission success. **(T-3)**

2.4.1.3. U. Failed to adequately lead or contribute to the mission planning effort. Failed to comply with procedures prescribed in applicable guidance manuals, instructions, and/or directives contributed to significant deficiencies in mission execution/accomplishment. Failed to lead or participate in all required briefings and/or planning meetings without appropriate approval. **(T-3)**

2.4.2.  AREA 2, Systems and Equipment Knowledge (M)

2.4.2.1.  Q. Demonstrated thorough knowledge of network traffic flow, architecture, system component(s)/equipment, limitations, performance characteristics and operating procedures.  Correctly identified and located applicable components/equipment and determined operational status of system.  Properly configured system components/equipment.  Correctly identified and applied proper action(s) for system/equipment malfunctions.  Followed all applicable system/equipment operating directives, guides, manuals etc. **(T-3)**

2.4.2.2.  Q-. Minor deficiencies in demonstrating knowledge of network traffic flow, architecture, system component(s)/equipment, limitations, performance characteristics, or operating procedures but sufficient to perform the mission safely.  Able to identify and locate components/equipment with minor errors.  Slow to identify malfunctions and/or apply corrective actions with minor errors, omissions, or deviations.  Followed all system/equipment operating directives, guides, manuals...etc. with minor errors, omissions, or deviations.  Did not damage system/components/equipment or cause mission failure. **(T-3)**

2.4.2.3.  U. Demonstrated severe lack of knowledge of network traffic flow, architecture system component(s)/equipment, limitations, performance characteristics or operating procedures.  Unable to identify or failed to locate essential components/equipment.  Failed to identify malfunctions and/or apply corrective actions.  Failed to follow system/equipment operating directives, guides, manuals, etc., resulting in unsatisfactory employment and/or mission failure.  Poor procedures resulted in damage to system components/equipment and/or mission failure.

2.4.3.  AREA 3, Briefing (M)

2.4.3.1.  Q. Led or contributed to briefing effort as appropriate.  Utilized/followed local briefing guides, manuals and/or instructions.  The briefing was well organized and presented in a logical sequence, appropriate length, and professional manner.  Effectively incorporated briefing/training aids where applicable and effective techniques required for accomplishing the mission.  Briefed mission tasking/priorities, crew responsibilities/coordination, weapon system employment/sensor management, de-confliction contracts, and mission package integration (as applicable). Accurately briefed the current situational awareness status.  Crewmembers clearly understood roles, responsibilities, and mission requirements.  Was prepared at briefing time. **(T-3)**

2.4.3.2.  Q-. Led or contributed to briefing effort with minor errors/omissions/deviations.  Utilized/followed local briefing guides, manuals and/or instructions with minor deviations.  Briefing anomalies had minor impact on mission effectiveness but did not jeopardize mission success. **(T-3)**

2.4.3.3.  U. Inadequate leadership or participation in briefing development and/or presentation.  Did not utilize/follow local briefing guides, manuals and/or instructions.  Disorganized and/or confusing presentation.  Ineffective use of briefing/training aids.  Failed to brief mission tasking/priorities, crew responsibilities/coordination, weapon system employment/sensor management, de-confliction contracts, and mission package integration (as applicable). Failed to present major training events.  Failed to present an accurate situational awareness picture; not prepared at briefing time. **(T-3)**

2.4.4.  AREA 4, Positional Changeover Brief (M)

2.4.4.1. Q. Outgoing crewmember prepared and conducted a comprehensive positional changeover briefing with the oncoming crewmember IAW crew aid(s) and/or applicable directives. Reviewed factors, conditions, and the current operational/tactical situation for all Defensive Cyberspace Operations (DCO) missions, packages, sorties, etc. with the oncoming crew member and ensured items necessary for the effective conduct of tasked missions were understood by the oncoming crewmember. Minor errors/omissions/deviations did not impact mission effectiveness. Verified review of all Cybercrew Information File (CIF) Vol 1, Part B items and complied with Go/No-Go procedures prior to mission start.  Oncoming crewmember was attentive and asked questions as applicable to ensure mission effectiveness/accomplishment. **(T-3)**

2.4.4.2. Q-. Outgoing crewmember prepared and conducted a positional changeover briefing with minor errors/omissions/deviations using crew aid(s) and applicable directives.  Changeover briefing anomalies had minor impact on mission effectiveness but did not jeopardize mission success.  Oncoming crew member's level of attentiveness during changeover led to minor mission impact but did not jeopardize overall mission success. **(T-3)**

2.4.4.3. U. Outgoing crewmember failed to prepare and conduct an effective positional changeover briefing with the oncoming crewmember and/or failed to use appropriate crew aid(s) and applicable directives. Changeover briefing contained errors/omissions/deviations that could have significantly detracted from mission effectiveness and/or jeopardized mission success.  Failed to review CIF and/or comply with Go/No-Go procedures. Oncoming crew member's lack of attentiveness significantly detracted from mission effectiveness and/or jeopardized mission success. **(T-3)**

2.4.5.  AREA 5, Pre-Sortie Check Procedures (M)

2.4.5.1. Q. Performed all mission/operations checks as required IAW applicable guides and/or crew aids.  Adequately ensured, determined, and/or verified weapon system operational state and cybercrew readiness prior to on-watch period or entering tasked vulnerability period.  Ensured crew understanding of most up-to-date tasking(s) prior to on-watch or vulnerability period execution.  Deviated from crew aids and/or omitted steps only when appropriate and was able to substantiate justification.  Minor errors/deviations/omissions did not detract from mission efficiencies nor jeopardize mission success. **(T-3)**

2.4.5.2. Q-. Minor errors/omissions occurred without justification but did not jeopardize overall mission success. **(T-3)**

2.4.5.3. U.  Did not perform mission/operations checks.  Failed to determine/verify weapon system operational state and cybercrew readiness prior to on-watch period or entering tasked vulnerability period.  Did not utilize any crew aids and/or utilized wrong crew aids.  Errors/deviations/omissions contributed to jeopardizing mission success. **(T-3)**

2.4.6.  AREA 6, Situational Awareness (C)

2.4.6.1.  Q.  Conducted the mission with a sense of understanding/comprehension and in a timely, efficient manner. Anticipated situations which would have adversely affected the mission and made appropriate decisions based on available information. Maintained overall good situational awareness. Recognized temporary loss of situational awareness in self or others and took appropriate action to regain awareness without detracting from mission accomplishment or jeopardizing safety. **(T-3)**

2.4.6.2.  U.  Decisions or lack thereof resulted in failure to accomplish the assigned mission. Demonstrated poor judgment or loss of situational awareness. **(T-3)**

2.4.7.  AREA 7, Safety (C)

2.4.7.1.  Q.  Aware of and complied with all factors required for safe operations and mission accomplishment. **(T-3)**

2.4.7.2.  U.  Unaware of safety factors or disregarded procedures to safely operate the weapon system and/or conduct the mission.  Conducted unsafe actions that jeopardized mission accomplishment and/or put crewmembers at risk of injury or death.  Operated in a manner that could or did result in damage to the weapon system/equipment. **(T-3)**

2.4.8.  AREA 8, Emergency Procedures and Equipment (M)

2.4.8.1.  Q.  Demonstrated/explained thorough knowledge of location and proper use of emergency equipment.  Demonstrated/explained effective coordination of emergency actions with other crewmembers without delay or confusion.  Followed appropriate crew aids as required.  Minor errors did not impact efficiencies in addressing the emergency. (This area may be evaluated orally.) **(T-3)**

2.4.8.2.  Q-.  Recognized emergency situations or malfunctions but slow to demonstrate/explain appropriate response actions.  Examinee demonstrated/explained correct procedures with minor errors and/or was slow to locate equipment and/or appropriate crew aids.  Slow or hesitant to demonstrate/explain effective coordination of emergency actions with other crewmembers.  Minor crew aids errors/omissions/deviations caused minor inefficiencies addressing the emergency situation/malfunction but did not exacerbate the situation. **(T-3)**

2.4.8.3.  U.  Failed to recognize emergency situations or malfunctions.  Failed to demonstrate/explain proper response actions.  Failed to demonstrate/explain knowledge of location or proper use of emergency equipment or crew aids.  Failed to demonstrate/explain coordination of emergency actions with other crewmembers.  Crew aids errors/omissions/deviations contributed to ineffective actions or exacerbating an emergency situation and/or malfunction. **(T-3)**

2.4.9.  AREA 9, Crew Discipline (C)

2.4.9.1.  Q.  Demonstrated strict professional crew discipline throughout all phases of the mission. Planned, briefed, executed, and debriefed mission in accordance with applicable instructions and directives. **(T-3)**

2.4.9.2.  U. Failed to demonstrate strict professional crew discipline throughout all phases of the mission.  Violated or failed to comply with applicable instructions and directives which could have jeopardized safety of crewmembers or mission accomplishment. **(T-3)**

2.4.10.  AREA 10, Crew Coordination (M)

2.4.10.1.  Q. Effectively coordinated with other crewmembers and/or teams during all phases of the mission enabling efficient, well-coordinated actions. Demonstrated knowledge of other crewmembers' duties and responsibilities. Proactively provided direction and/or information to the crew; communicated in a clear and effective manner, actively sought other crewmember opinions and/or ideas, and asked for or provided constructive feedback as necessary. **(T-3)**

2.4.10.2.  Q-. Some breakdowns in communication but did not detract from overall mission success. Demonstrated limited knowledge of other crewmembers' and/or teams' duties/responsibilities. Unclear communication at times caused confusion and/or limited crew/team interaction.  Some unnecessary prompting required from other crewmembers. **(T-3)**

2.4.10.3.  U. Severe breakdowns in coordination precluded mission effectiveness, resulted in mission failure or jeopardized safety of crewmembers or teams.  Lacked basic knowledge of other crewmembers' and/or teams' duties and responsibilities. Unclear/lack of communication or excessive prompting required by crewmembers or teams put mission and/or safety of others at risk. **(T-3)**

2.4.11.  AREA 11, Communication (M)

2.4.11.1.  Q. Timely and effective communication with external agencies and/or mission partners when required.  Concise and accurate information passed using proper medium, terminology, format and/or brevity IAW applicable crew aids.  Sound understanding and use of voice, email, chat, and collaborative tools to communicate mission essential information.  Demonstrated a thorough understanding of Operations Security (OPSEC) procedures. **(T-3)**

2.4.11.2.  Q-. Minor errors/deviations/omissions in communications with external agencies and/or mission partners that did not detract from overall mission accomplishment.  Limited understanding and use of voice, email, chat, and collaborative tools.  Demonstrated limited understanding of OPSEC procedures with minor errors or deviations that did not jeopardize mission accomplishment.  Deviated from applicable crew aids but did not cause mission failure. **(T-3)**

2.4.11.3.  U. Severe breakdowns in communication with external agencies and/or mission partners precluded mission effectiveness/failure or jeopardized safety of others. Unclear/inaccurate information passed or improper/inadequate use of medium, terminology, format, and/or brevity put mission accomplishment at risk.  Significant OPSEC errors or deviations jeopardized mission accomplishment.  Did not use crew aids. **(T-3)**

2.4.12.  AREA 12, Task Management (M)

2.4.12.1.  Q. Accurately identified, effectively prioritized, and/or efficiently managed the tasks based on all information.  Used available resources to manage workload, communicated task priorities to other crew members and/or internal teams. Recognized and requested assistance from other crewmembers when task-saturated. Gathered/crosschecked available data and effectively identified alternatives when necessary. Clearly stated decisions and ensured they were understood. Investigated doubts and concerns of other crew members when necessary. **(T-3)**

2.4.12.2. Q-. Identified, prioritized, and managed tasks with minor omissions and/or errors which did not affect safety of crewmembers or effective mission accomplishment. Limited use of available resources to manage workload and/or did not completely communicate task priorities to other crew members and/or internal teams. Slow to recognize task saturation and/or request assistance from crewmembers. Made minor errors in identifying contingencies, gathering data, or communicating a decision but did not affect safe or effective mission accomplishment. **(T-3)**

2.4.12.3. U. Failed to identify, prioritize, or manage essential tasks leading to possible unsafe conditions or significant risk to mission accomplishment. Failed to communicate task priorities to other crew members and/or internal teams. Improperly or unable to identify contingencies, gather data, or communicate decisions putting mission accomplishment and/or safety of others at risk. Failed to recognize task overload or failed to seek assistance from other crewmembers which put at risk mission accomplishment or safety of crewmembers. **(T-3)**

2.4.13.  AREA 13, Reports, Logs and Forms (M)

2.4.13.1. Q. Recognized all situations meeting reporting criteria. When required, provided timely, accurate, and correctly formatted reports [e.g. Tactical Reports (TACREPs), Situation Reports (SITREPs), Mission Reports (MISREPs)] or inputs to mission-related information management portals/collaborative information sharing environments. All required logs [i.e. Master Station Log (MSL)], media and forms were complete, accurate, legible, and accomplished on time and IAW with applicable directives, tasking, and policy. Information was provided in sufficient detail to allow accurate and timely analysis of associated data. Complied with security procedures and directives. **(T-3)**

2.4.13.2. Q-. Minor errors/ deviations/omissions/latency on required reports, logs, media, or forms led to minor inefficiencies but did not affect conduct of the mission. Complied with security procedures and directives. **(T-3)**

2.4.13.3. U. Failed to recognize situations meeting reporting criteria and/or failed to report events essential to mission accomplishment. Major errors/deviations/omissions/latency in accomplishing logs, reports/inputs, media, or forms precluded effective mission accomplishment or analysis of mission data. Failed to comply with security procedures and directives. **(T-3)**

2.4.14.  AREA 14, Crew Debrief (M)

2.4.14.1. Q. Debriefed the mission thoroughly or contributed to the briefing content to ensure it included all pertinent items. Reconstructed operational events, compared results with initial objectives for the mission, debriefed deviations, and provided individual crew member feedback as appropriate. Organized IAW guidance/directives and professionally presented in a logical sequence using available briefing aids. Summarized lessons learned and ensured they were documented. Provided crew commander/operations controller with applicable input on all required mission/crew/system-related events, including mission log/report/database information for inclusion in the crew debrief. Used applicable crew aid(s) as required. Minor errors/omissions/deviations did not impact debrief effectiveness or efficiencies. **(T-3)**

2.4.14.2. Q-. Led or contributed to debriefing effort with minor errors/omissions/deviations. Some events out of sequence with some unnecessary redundancy. **(T-3)**

2.4.14.3. U. Inadequate leadership or participation in debrief. Disorganized and/or confusing debriefing presentation. Ineffective use of briefing/training aids. Failed to reconstruct operational events, compare results with initial objectives for the mission, debrief deviations, and/or offer corrective guidance as appropriate. Absent from debrief (whole or in-part) without appropriate supervisor approval. **(T-3)**

2.4.15. AREA 15, Composite Force (CF) / Mutual Support (MS) (M)

2.4.15.1. Q. Effectively planned and leveraged CF support, MS agencies, and/or internal/external teams when needed. **(T-3)**

2.4.15.2. Q-. Limited planning and/or leverage of CF support or MS agency support contributed to confusion among all or some agencies/teams. Less than optimum mission efficiency, however overall mission success was not jeopardized. **(T-3)**

2.4.15.3. U. Inadequate or incorrect planning/leverage of CF support, MS agency support, and/or internal/external team support, resulted in mission failure. Did not leverage support when needed. **(T-3)**

**2.5. AFINC Operator SMQ Evaluation Criteria.**

2.5.1. AREA 16, Cyberspace Collection (M)

2.5.1.1. Q. Effective and timely execution resulted in prompt collection of relevant data and information from targeted terrain IAW tasking. **(T-3)**

2.5.1.2. Q-. Minor errors caused less than optimal data and information collection from the targeted terrain resulting in minor data loss. **(T-3)**

2.5.1.3. U. Major errors delayed or prevented data and information collection and/or resulted in data and information collection failure. Collected information was not related to targeted terrain and/or tasking. **(T-3)**

2.5.2. AREA 17, Cyberspace Strike (M)

2.5.2.1. Q. Effectively, degraded, disrupted, denied, or destroyed adversary activity in a timely and effective manner IAW all ROEs and given restrictions. **(T-3)**

2.5.2.2. Q-. Minor errors in execution led to slower than desired performance in degrading, disrupting, denying or destroying adversary activity. Required ample assistance from other crew members to complete the mission but did not affect overall mission success. **(T-3)**

2.5.2.3. U. Failed to degrade, disrupt, deny, or destroy adversary activity in a timely and effective manner. IAW all ROEs and given restrictions. Errors in execution caused a major delay in the mission execution window or prevented mission accomplishment. **(T-3)**

2.5.3. AREA 18, Cyberspace Control (M)

2.5.3.1. Q. Effective coordination with outside agency(s) and timely execution resulted in prompt access and/or network freedom of maneuver for supported cyberspace forces IAW tasking, ROEs and restrictions without errors. **(T-3)**

2.5.3.2. Q-. Remained IAW tasking but minor errors and/or less than optimal coordination with cyberspace partner(s) caused access and/or freedom of maneuver delays for supported cyberspace forces but did not cause mission failure. **(T-3)**

2.5.3.3. U. Major errors delayed or prevented execution, access or network freedom of maneuver. Employment/engagement was outside the tasking and/or caused mission failure. **(T-3)**

2.5.4. AREA 19, Weapon System Threat Correlation/Analysis (M)

2.5.4.1. Q. Properly planned and executed collection, correlation and categorization of network security events IAW tasking, directives, and applicable checklists. Demonstrated thorough knowledge of procedures and techniques for reviewing alerts, query results and analyzing data to identify potential malicious traffic. Correctly recognized, identified, and categorized suspicious activities/events requiring further analysis and investigation. Effectively differentiated between events and incidents. Effectively correlated intelligence indicators with observed network activity and analyzed data to identify weapon system impact. **(T-3)**

2.5.4.2. Q-. Minor errors, omissions, or delays detracted from mission efficiency but did not jeopardize overall mission accomplishment. **(T-3)**

2.5.4.3. U. Errors, omissions, or delays jeopardized overall mission accomplishment. **(T-3)**

## Chapter 3

## INSTRUCTOR EVALUATIONS AND GRADING CRITERIA

**3.1. General.** Grading criteria contained herein cannot accommodate every situation. Written parameters must be tempered with sortie objectives, evaluator judgment, and task accomplishment in the determination of overall aircrew performance. **(T-2)**

**3.2. Instructor Upgrade and Qualification Requisites** . Prior to an initial Instructor Evaluation, Instructor examinees must complete all requisites for Instructor upgrade consideration, nomination and training IAW AFI 17-202V1, AFI 17-2AFINCV1, and all applicable supplemental guidance. **(T-2)**

**3.3. Instructor Qualification Evaluations** : When possible, units should strive to combine instructor evaluations (initial and recurring/periodic) with periodic QUAL evaluations. Instructor evaluations can only be combined with QUAL evaluations when the examinee is in their periodic QUAL eligibility period. There is no eligibility period associated with an Instructor Qualification, however, Instructor qualifications will expire after the 17$^{th}$ month from the previous Instructor Qualification Evaluation. See paragraph 3.5 for documentation guidance. **(T-2)**

3.3.1. Initial Instructor evaluations should be conducted with a student occupying the applicable cybercrew position whenever possible. Recurring or periodic Instructor Evaluations may be conducted with the SEE role playing as the student. **(T-2)**

3.3.2. The instructor examinee will monitor all phases of the mission from an advantageous position and be prepared to demonstrate or explain any area or procedure. The SEE will particularly note the instructor's ability to recognize student difficulties and provide effective, timely instruction and/or corrective action. The SEE should also evaluate the grade assigned and the completed grade sheet or event training form for the student on all initial instructor checks. **(T-2)**

3.3.3. The student will perform those duties prescribed by the instructor for the mission/sortie being accomplished. If an actual student is not available, the SEE will identify to the examinee (prior to the mission) the level of performance expected from the SEE acting as the student. If this option is utilized, at least one event or briefing must be instructed. **(T-2)**

3.3.4. Periodic instructor evaluations will be administered in conjunction with required periodic qualification evaluations. The examinee must occupy the primary duty position for an adequate period of time to demonstrate proficiency in the crew position with required qualification evaluations. All instructor evaluations will include a pre-mission and post-mission briefing. **(T-2)**

3.3.5. Awarding a "U" in any of the Instructor Grading Criteria areas will result in a Q-3 for the overall instructor grade. The overall grade for the instructor portion of the evaluation will be no higher than the lowest overall grade awarded under QUAL. **(T-2)**

**3.4. Instructor Evaluation Grading Criteria** . All Instructor Evaluation Criteria must be observed and graded to ensure a complete evaluation. **(T-2)** Specific requirements for each evaluation are as follows:

3.4.1. AREA 20, Instructional Ability (M)

3.4.1.1. Q. Demonstrated ability to effectively communicate weapon system capability, mission planning, briefing/debriefing, employment/ Tactics, Tips and Procedures (TTP), and tasked mission areas to the student. Provided appropriate corrective guidance when necessary. Planned ahead and made timely decisions. Correctly analyzed student errors. **(T-2)**

3.4.1.2. Q-. Demonstrated a limited ability to effectively communicate weapon system capability, mission planning, briefing/debriefing, employment/TTP, and tasked mission areas to the student. Provided corrective guidance with some errors. Demonstrated limited ability to plan ahead and made some timely decisions. Correctly analyzed some, but not all student errors. **(T-2)**

3.4.1.3. U. Unable to effectively communicate with the student. Did not provide corrective action where necessary. Did not plan ahead or anticipate student problems. Incorrectly analyzed student errors. Adversely impacted student progress. **(T-2)**

3.4.2. AREA 21, Instructional Briefings/Critique (M)

3.4.2.1. Q. Briefings were well organized, accurate, and thorough. Reviewed student's present level of training and defined mission events to be performed. Demonstrated ability during critique to reconstruct the mission/sortie, offer mission analysis, and provide corrective guidance where appropriate. Completed all training documents according to prescribed directives. Awarded appropriate grades. **(T-2)**

3.4.2.2. Q-. Most briefings were organized, accurate, and thorough. Reviewed student's present level of training and defined most mission events to be performed. Demonstrated limited ability during critique to reconstruct the mission/sortie, offer mission analysis, and provide corrective guidance where appropriate. Completed some training documents according to prescribed directives. Awarded appropriate grades for some events. **(T-2)**

3.4.2.3. U. Pre-mission or post-mission briefings were marginal or nonexistent. Did not review student's training folder or past performance. Failed to adequately critique student or conducted an incomplete mission analysis which compromised learning. Student strengths or weaknesses were not identified. Adversely impacted student progress. Inappropriate grades awarded. Overlooked or omitted major discrepancies. **(T-2)**

3.4.3. AREA 22, Demonstration and Performance (M)

3.4.3.1. Q-. Effectively demonstrated procedures and techniques. Demonstrated thorough knowledge of weapon system/components, procedures, and all applicable publications and regulations. **(T-2)**

3.4.3.2. Q-. Limited ability to demonstrate procedures and techniques. Demonstrated limited knowledge of weapon system/components, procedures, and all applicable publications and regulations. **(T-2)**

3.4.3.3. U. Did not demonstrate correct procedure or technique. Insufficient depth of knowledge about weapon system/components, procedures, or proper source material. Adversely impacted student progress. **(T-2)**

**3.5. Instructor Evaluation Documentation** .

3.5.1. Instructor Qualification Evaluations will be documented as a SPOT evaluation on the AF Form 4418 and AF Form 4420, *Individual's Record of Duties and Qualifications* and maintained in the member's cyber crew qualification folder IAW AFI 17-202V2, applicable higher headquarters supplements, and local supplemental guidance. **(T-2)**   Additional Instructor Evaluation documentation is as follows:

3.5.2. Initial Instructor Qualification Evaluation.

3.5.2.1. If conducted in conjunction with the Instructor Examinee's periodic QUAL evaluation, the Instructor Qualification Evaluation will be documented on the same AF Form 4418, placing SPOT in the second "Evaluation Type" block of Section II Qualification below annotating QUAL.  Place a statement in Section V Comments that the QUAL evaluation was in conjunction with an Initial Instructor Qualification Evaluation.  Place any comments specific to the Instructor portion of the evaluation separately from the QUAL portion of the evaluation. **(T-2)**

3.5.2.2. If the Instructor Qualification Evaluation is not in conjunction with a periodic QUAL evaluation, document the evaluation as a SPOT in the first "Evaluation Type" block of Section II Qualification and place a statement in Section V Comments that the evaluation was an Initial Instructor Qualification Evaluation. Place any comments regarding commendable performance and/or discrepancies for the instructor evaluation in Section V Comments. **(T-2)**

3.5.2.3. Upon completion of the AF Form 4418, place the appropriate corresponding entry on the AF Form 4420. **(T-3)**

3.5.3. Recurring/Periodic Instructor Qualification Evaluation.

3.5.3.1. If conducted in conjunction with the Instructor Examinee's periodic QUAL evaluation, the Instructor Qualification Evaluation will be documented on the same AF Form 4418, placing SPOT in the second "Evaluation Type" block of Section II Qualification below annotating QUAL.  Place a statement in Section V Comments that the evaluation was a periodic QUAL evaluation in conjunction with periodic or recurring Instructor Qualification Evaluation.  Place any comments specific to the Instructor portion of the evaluation separately from the QUAL portion of the evaluation. **(T-2)**

3.5.3.2. If the Instructor Qualification Evaluation is not in conjunction with a periodic QUAL evaluation, document the evaluation as a SPOT in the first "Evaluation Type" block of Section II Qualification and place a statement in Section V Comments that the evaluation was recurring or periodic Instructor Qualification Evaluation. Place any comments regarding commendable performance and/or discrepancies for the instructor evaluation in Section V Comments. **(T-2)**

3.5.3.3. Upon completion of the AF Form 4418, place the appropriate corresponding entry on the AF Form 4420. **(T-2)**

3.5.4. Letter of Certification (Letter of Xs).

3.5.4.1. Upon the successful completion of an Instructor Qualification Evaluation, units will ensure the crewmembers instructor status is reflected on the Letter of Xs. **(T-2)**

3.5.4.2. Upon the expiration of a qualification or failure of an Instructor Qualification Evaluation, units will ensure the crewmembers instructor status is reflected on the Letter of Xs. **(T-2)**

**Chapter 4**

**SEE OBJECTIVITY EVALUATIONS AND GRADING CRITERIA**

**4.1. General.** SEE Objectivity Evaluations are a vehicle for commanders to upgrade crewmembers for SEE qualification and a tool to monitor the evaluator crew force's adherence to Stan/Eval directives. Grading criteria contained herein cannot accommodate every situation. Written parameters must be tempered with sortie objectives, evaluator judgment, and task accomplishment in the determination of overall examinee performance. The criteria contained in this chapter are established by experience, policies, and procedures set forth in weapon system manuals and other directives. The criteria contained in this chapter are applicable to all SEE Objectivity Evaluations for AFINC crewmembers. **(T-2)**

**4.2. Evaluator Upgrade and Qualification Requisites** . Evaluator upgrade candidates will be selected from the most qualified and competent instructors. **(T-2)**

4.2.1. SEE Upgrade candidate nominations will be approved by the unit commander in writing. Once approved, candidates must complete all SEE training IAW AFI 17-202V2, this instruction, and all applicable supplemental guidance. **(T-2)** As a minimum, SEE training will consist of:

4.2.1.1. Local SEE academics/instruction covering all Stan/Eval programs and procedures. Training completion should be documented on active duty Group/Stan/Eval crew aids along with a signed certificate from the weapon system's OG/CC or OG/CD. SEE upgrade packages will be maintained in the unit Stan/Eval office. **(T-2)**

4.2.1.2. The candidate observing one entire evaluation performed by a qualified SEE. NOTE:  To the maximum extent possible, SEE Upgrade candidates should observe evaluations conducted within the weapon system for which they are qualified, however when not practical, the observed evaluation may be conducted with a qualified SEE in the same Group regardless of weapon system or crew position. Training completion should be documented on locally developed OG/CC crew aids and maintained in the unit Stan/Eval office. **(T-2)**

4.2.1.3. Completion of a SEE Objectivity Evaluation under the supervision of a qualified SEE. NOTE:  The SEE Objectivity Evaluation will be conducted within the weapon system and crew position for which the SEE Upgrade candidate (SEE Examinee) maintains qualification. See paragraph 4.5 for SEE Objectivity Evaluation (AF Form 4418) documentation guidance. **(T-2)**

**4.3. SEE Objectivity Evaluations** . There is no eligibility period or expiration date associated with a SEE Objectivity Evaluation. Once obtained, crewmembers maintain SEE qualification unless they fail a QUAL evaluation, fail an Instructor evaluation, fail a SEE Objectivity Evaluation, their weapon system QUAL expires, or upon their SEE appointment being revoked/rescinded by the appointing official. See paragraph 4.5. for SEE Objectivity Evaluation documentation guidance. **(T-2)**

4.3.1. Only a qualified cyberspace weapon system SEE may administer a SEE Objectivity Evaluation to a cyberspace SEE examinee. SEE Objectivity Evaluations may be administered by SEE Examiners that are qualified in a different cyberspace weapon system type or crew position from the SEE examinee. NOTE: This is common when the SEE Objectivity Evaluation is in conjunction with a higher headquarters inspection. **(T-2)**

4.3.2. Members receiving a SEE Objectivity Evaluations will not combined any other type of evaluation affecting their positional status. **(T-2)**

4.3.3. SEE Objectivity Evaluations will ensure the SEE examinee (for example in the case of a SEE Objectivity conducted as part of a higher headquarters inspection) observes and grades the entire mission activity of the QUAL examinee. Mission activity is defined as all mission planning, briefing, execution, and debrief activities for the mission/sortie. **(T-2)**

4.3.4. The SEE Upgrade candidate or SEE Examinee will brief the qualified SEE Examiner on all observations, grades, commendable/discrepancies (if any), recommended additional training, and other mission related debrief topics prior to debriefing the QUAL examinee and/or examinee's supervisor. **(T-2)**

4.3.5. The SEE Upgrade candidate or SEE Examinee will complete the AF Form 4418 and have the SEE Examiner review it for completeness and accuracy. The SEE Examiner's signature block and signature (not signature/block of the SEE Upgrade candidate or SEE Examinee) will be entered on the AF Form 4418. **(T-2)**

4.3.6. The SEE Examiner will administer a pre-brief and debrief to the SEE Examinee. **(T-2)**

4.3.7. For SEE Upgrade candidates, SEE Objectivity evaluations will only be administered for observed INIT QUAL or periodic QUAL evaluations. Additionally, the QUAL evaluation may not be combined with an Instructor Evaluation. **(T-2)**

**4.4. SEE Objectivity Evaluation Grading Criteria** . All SEE Objectivity Evaluation Criteria must be observed and graded to ensure a complete evaluation. The following grading criteria will be used by SEE's when conducting SEE Objectivity Evaluations. A grade of Q- requiring additional training or a grade of U in any area for the SEE Objectivity Examinee will require an overall rating of "3". Cumulative deviations will be considered when determining the overall rating of either "1" or "3". **(T-2)** Specific requirements for each evaluation are as follows:

4.4.1. AREA 23, Compliance with Directives (M)

4.4.1.1. Q. Complied with all operational directives and guidance. Complied with all directives pertaining to the administration of a positional and/or instructor evaluation. **(T-2)**

4.4.1.2. Q-. Complied with most directives. Deviations did not jeopardize the mission, the effectiveness of the evaluation, or crew safety. **(T-2)**

4.4.1.3. U. Failure to comply with directives jeopardized mission effectiveness, effectiveness of the evaluation, and/or crew safety. **(T-2)**

4.4.2. AREA 24, Stan/Eval Examiner (SEE) Briefing (M)

4.4.2.1. Q. Thoroughly briefed the examinee on the conduct of the evaluation, mission requirements, responsibilities, grading criteria, and examiner actions/position during the evaluation. **(T-3)**

4.4.2.2. Q-. Items were omitted during the briefing causing minor confusion. Did not fully brief the examinee as to the conduct and purpose of the evaluation. **(T-2)**

4.4.2.3. U. Examiner failed to adequately brief the examinee. **(T-2)**

4.4.3. AREA 25, Performance Assessment and Grading (M)

4.4.3.1. Q. Identified all discrepancies and assigned proper area grade. Awarded the appropriate overall grade based on the examinee's performance. **(T-2)**

4.4.3.2. Q-. Most discrepancies were identified. Failed to assign Q- grade when appropriate. Assigned discrepancies for performance which was within standards. Awarded an overall grade without consideration of cumulative deviations in the examinee's performance. **(T-2)**

4.4.3.3. U. Failed to identify most discrepancies. Did not award a grade commensurate with overall performance. Failed to assign additional training when warranted. **(T-2)**

4.4.4. AREA 26, Additional Training Assignment (M)

4.4.4.1. Q. Assigned proper additional training when warranted. *NOTE:* If the QUAL Examinee's performance (i.e. Q1) does not warrant the assignment of additional training, the SEE Examinee will verbally explain to the SEE Examiner the proper procedures for assigning additional training. This may be accomplished as part of the SEE Objectivity pre-brief or debrief. **(T-2)**

4.4.4.2. Q-. Additional training assigned was insufficient to ensure the examinee would achieve proper level of qualification. SEE Examinee's discrepancy or omission was correctable prior to QUAL Examinee debrief and in the SEE Objectivity debrief. **(T-2)**

4.4.4.3. U. Failed to assign additional training when warranted. **(T-2)**

4.4.5. AREA 27, Examinee Critique / Debrief (M)

4.4.5.1. Q. Thoroughly debriefed the examinee on all aspects of the evaluation. Reconstructed and debriefed all key mission events, providing instruction and references to directives and guidance when applicable. **(T-2)**

4.4.5.2. Q-. Some errors/omissions in reconstructing key mission events, in discussing deviations/discrepancies, referencing directives/guidance and debriefing of assigned grades. Did not advise the examinee of all additional training when warranted. Errors/omissions did not adversely affect overall evaluation effectiveness. **(T-2)**

4.4.5.3. U. Failed to discuss any assigned area grades or the overall rating. Changed grades without briefing the examinee and/or supervisor. Did not debrief key mission events and/or provide appropriate instruction during critique. **(T-2)**

4.4.6. AREA 28, Supervisor Debrief (M)

4.4.6.1. Q. Thoroughly debriefed the QUAL Examinee's Supervisor. Reconstructed and debriefed all key mission events pertinent to the QUAL Examinee's performance, citing references to directives and guidance when applicable. Briefed the supervisor on all discrepancies requiring additional training, downgraded areas, and the overall qualification rating being assigned to the QUAL Examinee. *NOTE:* If the QUAL Examinee's performance (i.e. Q1) does not warrant a supervisor debrief, the SEE

Examinee will verbally explain to the SEE Examiner the proper procedures for conducting a supervisor debriefing.  This may be accomplished as part of the SEE Objectivity pre-brief or debrief. **(T-2)**

4.4.6.2. Q-. Some errors/omissions in reconstructing key mission events, discussing deviations/discrepancies, referencing directives/guidance, debriefing of assigned additional training, and assigning of QUAL Examinee grades/ratings with the supervisor. Errors/omissions did not adversely affect overall evaluation effectiveness. **(T-2)**

4.4.6.3. U. Failed to discuss any observed discrepancies, assigned area downgrades or the overall rating with the supervisor. Changed grades without briefing the examinee and/or supervisor.  Did not debrief key mission events contributing to the QUAL examinees overall performance and assigned qualification rating. **(T-2)**

4.4.7.  AREA 29, SEE Performance and Evaluation Documentation (M)

4.4.7.1. Q. SEE Examinee performed as briefed and ensured a thorough evaluation of the QUAL and/or Instructor (INSTR) evaluation examinee.  SEE Examinee correctly documented the QUAL or INSTR Examinee's performance on the AF Form 4418. **(T-2)**

4.4.7.2. Q-. Minor errors or discrepancies during the mission did not impact or detract from the QUAL or INSTR Examinees' performance.  Minor errors/discrepancies in accomplishing documentation. **(T-2)**

4.4.7.3. U. Major errors/disruptions impacted or detracted from the QUAL or INSTR Examinee's performance and/or prevented a thorough evaluation.  Failure or major errors/discrepancies in accomplishing documentation. **(T-2)**

**4.5. SEE Objectivity Evaluation Documentation** .  SEE Objectivity Evaluations will be documented as a SPOT evaluation on the AF Form 4418 and AF Form 4420 and maintained in the member's cyber crew qualification folder IAW AFI 17-202V2 and applicable higher headquarters/local supplemental guidance.

4.5.1.  Letter of Certification (Letter of Xs).

4.5.1.1. Upon the successful completion of a SEE Objectivity Evaluation, units will ensure the crewmembers SEE status is reflected on the Letter of Xs. **(T-2)**

4.5.1.2. Upon the decertification or loss of SEE qualification, units will ensure the Letter of Xs appropriately reflects the crewmember's status. **(T-2)**

WILLIAM J. BENDER, Lt Gen, USAF
Chief, Information Dominance and
Chief Information Officer

**Attachment 1**

**GLOSSARY OF REFERENCES AND SUPPORTING INFORMATION**

*References*

Title 5, Privacy Act (5 U.S.C. § 552a), *The Freedom of Information Act*

Title 5 United States Code, *Section 552a (Privacy Act)*, update January 7, 2011

Privacy Act of 1974 authorized by 10 U.S.C. 8013

AFPD 17-2, *Cyberspace Operations,* April 12, 2016

AFI 17-202 V1, *Cybercrew Training,* April 2, 2014

AFI 17-202 V2, *Cybercrew Standardization and Evaluation,* October 15, 2014

AFI 17-202 V3, *Cyberspace Operations Procedures,* May 6, 2015

AFI 17-200, *General Cyberspace Operations,* February 15, 2014

AFI 17-2AFINCV1, *Air Force Intranet Network Control (AFNIC) Training*

AFI 17-2AFINCV3, *Air Force Intranet Network Control (AFINC) Operations and Procedures*

AFI 33-360, *Publications and Forms Management,* December 1, 2015

AFMAN 33-363, *Management of Records,* March 1, 2008 (*Incorporating Change 2, 9 June 2016, Certified Current 21 July 2016*)

*Adopted Forms*

AF Form 679, *Air Force Publication Compliance Item Waiver Request/Approval*

AF Form 847, *Recommendation for Change of Publication*

AF Form 4418, *Certificate of Cybercrew Qualification*

AF Form 4420, *Individual's Record of Duties and Qualifications*

*Abbreviations and Acronyms*

**AFI**—Air Force Instruction

**AFIN**—Air Force Information Network

**AFINC**—O AFINC Operator

**AFINC**—Air Force Intranet Control

**AFMAN**—Air Force Manual

**AFRC**—Air Force Reserve Command

**AFRIMS**—Air Force Records Management Information System

**AFSPC**—Air Force Space Command

**ANG**—Air National Guard

**CC**—Crew Commander

**CF**—Composite Force

**CIF**—Crew Information File

**CRM**—Crew Resource Management

**CTD**—Cyberspace Training Device

**DCO**— Defensive Cyberspace Operations

**EPE**—Emergency Procedure Evaluation

**HQ**—Headquarters

**IAW**—In Accordance With

**INSTR**—Instructor

**LEP**—List of Effective Pages

**MAJCOM**—Major Command

**MISREPs**—Mission Reports

**MS**—Mutual Support

**MSL**—Master Station Log

**MSN**—Mission Qualification

**TDY**—Temporary Duty

**NAF**—Numbered Air Force

**N/N**—No-notice

**OC**—Operations Controller

**OG**—Operations Group

**OG/CC**—Operations Group Commander

**OGV**—Operations Group Standardization/Evaluation

**OPR**—Office of Primary Responsibility

**OPSEC**—Operations Security

**QUAL**—Qualification

**RDS**—Air Force Records Disposition Schedule

**SEE**—Standardization and Evaluation Examiners

**SITREPs**—Situation Reports

**SMQ**—Special Mission Qualification

**SPOT**—Spot Evaluation

**SQ**—Squadron

**SQ/CC**—Squadron

**STAN/EVAL**—Standardization and Evaluation

**TACREPs**—Tactical Reports

**TDY**—Temporary Duty

**TTP**—Tactics, Tips and Procedures

**WG**—Wing

*Terms*

**AFINC—O** -- Cyberspace operator qualified to perform AF Intranet Control Operator duties

**Commendable**—An observed exemplary demonstration of knowledge and/or or noteworthy ability to perform by the examinee in a specific graded area/subarea, tactic, technique, procedure, and/or task.

**Crew Commander (CC)**—Cyberspace operator qualified to perform crew commander duties.

**Cyberspace Training Device**—Simulators and part-task trainers which emulate some or all of the prime mission system/weapon system.

**Deficiency**—Demonstrated level of knowledge or ability to perform is inadequate, insufficient, or does not meet required or expected proficiency.

**Deviation**—Performing an action not in compliance with current procedures, directives, or regulations. Non-compliance due to unusual or extenuating circumstances is not considered a deviation. In some cases, momentary deviations may be acceptable; however, cumulative deviations will be considered in determining the overall qualification level.

**Discrepancy**—Any observed deviations/errors/omissions, individually or cumulative, that detracts from the examinee's performance in obtaining a Q for a particular grading area/subarea.

**Error**—Non-compliance with a standard procedure. Performing incorrect actions or recording inaccurate information.

**Inadequate**—Lack or underutilization of available crew aids or resources to effectively/efficiently make operational and tactical decisions, gain/maintain situational awareness, or accomplish a task.

**Inappropriate**—Grades awarded are not consistent with observed performance.

**Instructor**—Crew member trained, qualified, and certified by the squadron commander as an instructor to perform both ground and in-flight training.

**Instructor Supervision**—When a current instructor, qualified in the same crew position, supervises a maneuver or training event.

**Major (deviation/error/omission)**—Detracted from task accomplishment, adversely affected use of equipment, or violated safety.

**Minor (deviation/error/omission)**—Did not detract from task accomplishment, adversely affect use of equipment, or violate safety.

**Omission**—To leave out a required action or annotation.

**Operations Controller (OC)**—Cyberspace operator qualified to perform operations controller duties.

**Stan/Eval Examiner (SEE)**—A crew member designated to administer evaluations.

**Supervised Training Status**—Crew member will perform weapon system duties under instructor supervision as designated by the squadron commander or evaluator.

*BY ORDER OF THE SECRETARY*
*OF THE AIR FORCE*

*AIR FORCE INSTRUCTION 17-2AFINC*
*VOLUME 3*

*23 MAY 2017*

*Cyberspace*

*AIR FORCE INTRANET NETWORK*
*CONTROL (AFINC) OPERATIONS*
*AND PROCEDURES*

**COMPLIANCE WITH THIS PUBLICATION IS MANDATORY**

**ACCESSIBILITY:** Publications and forms are available for downloading or ordering on the e- Publishing website at **www.e-Publishing.af.mil**

**RELEASABILITY:** There are no releasability restrictions on this publication

OPR: HQ USAF/A3CX/A6CX

Certified by: AF/A3C/A6C
(Col Donald J. Fielden)
Pages: 18

This volume implements Air Force (AF) Policy Directive (AFPD) 17-2, *Cyberspace Operations* and references AFI 17-202V3, *Cyberspace Operations and Procedures.* It applies to all Air Force Intranet Control (AFINC) units. This publication applies to all military and civilian AF personnel, members of the AF Reserve Command (AFRC), Air National Guard (ANG), and contractor support personnel in accordance with appropriate provisions contained in memoranda support agreements and AF contracts. This publication requires the collection and or maintenance of information protected by the Privacy Act (PA) of 1947. The authorities to collect and maintain the records prescribed in this publication are Title 10 United States Code, **Chapter 857** and Executive Order 9397, Numbering System for Federal Accounts Relating to Individual Persons, 30 November 1943, as amended by Executive Order 13478, Amendments to Executive Order 9397 Relating to Federal Agency Use of Social Security Numbers, November 18, 2008.

The authorities to waive wing/unit level requirements in this publication are identified with a Tier ("T-0, T-1, T-2, T-3") number following the compliance statement. See AFI 33-360, *Publications and Forms Management*, Table 1.1 for a description of the authorities associated with the Tier numbers. Submit requests for waivers through the chain of command to the appropriate Tier waiver approval authority, or alternately, to the publication OPR for non-tiered compliance items. Refer recommended changes and questions about this publication to the Office of Primary Responsibility (OPR) using AF Form 847, *Recommendation for Change of Publication*; route AF Forms 847 from the field through Major Command (MAJCOM) publications/forms managers to AF/A3C/A6C. Ensure that all records created as a result of processes prescribed in this publication are maintained IAW Air Force Manual (AFMAN) 33-363, *Management of Records*, and disposed of IAW the Air Force Records Disposition Schedule (RDS) in the Air Force Records Information Management System (AFRIMS).

**Chapter 1— GENERAL GUIDANCE**                                                                             **4**

    1.1.    References, Abbreviations, Acronyms, and Terms. See Attachment 1 .................   4

    1.2.    General. ...............................................................................................   4

    1.3.    Waivers. ..............................................................................................   4

    1.4.    Deviations. .........................................................................................   4

    1.5.    Processing Changes. ..........................................................................   4

    1.6.    Supplements. ......................................................................................   4

**Chapter 2— MISSION PLANNING**                                                                             **5**

    2.1.    Responsibilities. .................................................................................   5

    2.2.    Mission Planning Guidelines. ...........................................................   5

    2.3.    Briefings. ...........................................................................................   6

**Chapter 3— NORMAL OPERATING PROCEDURES**                                                                  **7**

    3.1.    Pre-Mission Arrival Times. ...............................................................   7

    3.2.    Crew Information File (CIF). .............................................................   7

    3.3.    Go/No-Go. ..........................................................................................   7

    3.4.    Unit-Developed Checklist/Local Crew Aids. (T-3) ...........................   8

    3.5.    Forms and Station Log. ......................................................................   8

    3.6.    Required Publications. .......................................................................   8

    3.7.    Operations Check (Ops Check). .........................................................   8

    3.8.    Abort/Knock-it-off. ...........................................................................   8

    3.9.    Dynamic Targeting. ...........................................................................   8

    3.10.    Dynamic Tasking. ............................................................................   9

    3.11.    Communications and Crew Coordination. ........................................   9

    3.12.    Mission Report (MISREP). ..............................................................   9

    3.13.    Crew Changeover. ............................................................................   9

3.14.    Positional Changeover Brief. ................................................................................ 10

3.15.    Debriefing. ............................................................................................................ 10

3.16.    Post Sortie Duties. ................................................................................................ 10

**Chapter 4— CREW DUTIES, RESPONSIBILITIES, AND PROCEDURES** **11**

4.1.    AFINC Responsibilities. ........................................................................................ 11

4.2.    Crew Stations. ....................................................................................................... 11

4.3.    Crew Duties. .......................................................................................................... 11

4.4.    Crew Positions. ..................................................................................................... 11

4.5.    Crew Qualification. ............................................................................................... 12

4.6.    New/Modified Equipment and/or Capabilities. .................................................... 12

4.7.    Crew Rest/Duty Period/Sortie Duration. .............................................................. 12

4.8.    Crew Scheduling. .................................................................................................. 13

**Attachment 1— GLOSSARY OF REFERENCES AND SUPPORTING INFORMATION** **14**

# Chapter 1

# GENERAL GUIDANCE

**1.1. References, Abbreviations, Acronyms, and Terms. See** Attachment 1

**1.2. General.** This volume, in conjunction with other governing directives, prescribes procedures for operating the AFINC weapon system under most circumstances. It is not a substitute for sound judgment or common sense. Procedures not specifically addressed may be accomplished if they enhance safe and effective mission accomplishment.

**1.3. Waivers.** Unless another approval authority is cited, waiver authority for this volume is MAJCOM/A3. Submit waiver requests using AF Form 679, *Air Force Publication Compliance Item Waiver Request/Approval.* Forward waiver requests through appropriate channels to the MAJCOM/A3 for approval. All approvals will include an expiration date. Waivers are issued for a maximum of one year from the effective date. **(T-2)**

**1.4. Deviations.** In the case of an urgent requirement or emergency the Crew Commander (AFINC/CC) will take appropriate action(s) to ensure safe operations. **(T-3)**

**1.5. Processing Changes.**

1.5.1. Submit recommended changes and questions about this publication through MAJCOM channels to the OPR using AF Form 847. **(T-2)**

1.5.2. The submitting MAJCOM will forward information copies of AF Forms 847 to all other MAJCOMS that use this publication. Using MAJCOMs will forward comments on AF Forms 847 to the OPR. **(T-2)**

1.5.3. OPR will:

1.5.3.1. Coordinate all changes to the basic instruction with affected MAJCOM/A3s.

1.5.3.2. Forward change recommendations to MAJCOM/A3for staffing and AF/A3 approval.

**1.6. Supplements.** Guidance for supplementing this publication is contained in AFI 33-360. These supplements will not duplicate, alter, amend or be less restrictive than the provisions of this instruction.

**Chapter 2**

**MISSION PLANNING**

**2.1. Responsibilities.** Individual crews, unit operations, and intelligence functions jointly share responsibility for mission planning. Crews will plan, brief and debrief all missions. The Crew Commander (AFINC/CC)/senior crew member is ultimately responsible for all aspects of mission planning to include complying with command guidance. Units may supplement mission planning requirements but will ensure an appropriate level of mission planning is conducted prior to each mission. **(T-3)**

**2.2. Mission Planning Guidelines.**

2.2.1. Effective mission accomplishment requires thorough mission planning and preparation. Specific mission planning elements are addressed in Air Force Tactics, Techniques, and Procedures (AFTTP) 3-1.General Planning, AFTTP 3-1.AFINC, Air Force Cyber Command (AFCYBER) and Joint Forces Headquarters-Cyber (JFHQ-C) AFCYBER Tactical Mission Planning, Briefing and Debriefing Guide, and any local crew aids. While not directive, these manuals are authoritative and useful in ensuring adequate mission planning and employment. **(T-3)**

2.2.2. Standard Operating Procedures (SOP). The squadron commander (SQ/CC), or delegate, is the approval authority for squadron standards. Operations group commander (OG/CC) may publish and approve group standards. The operations group Standardization and Evaluation office (OGV) will review all standards for compliance with AFI 17-series guidance. **(T-3)**

2.2.3. SQ/CC will provide adequate time and facilities for mission planning. Crews will accomplish sufficient planning to ensure successful mission accomplishment. Units will maintain facilities where all information and materials required for mission planning are available. The following mission planning areas will be considered prior to mission execution: Mission, Environment, Enemy, Effects, Capabilities, Plan, Phasing, Contracts, or Contingencies (ME3C-[PC]$^2$). **(T-3)**

2.2.4. The following mission information should be covered by the mission planners during planning:

2.2.4.1. Tasking Order and line number (if applicable) **(T-3)**

2.2.4.2. Minimum forces **(T-3)**

2.2.4.3. Terrain **(T-3)**

2.2.4.4. Communication plan **(T-3)**

2.2.4.5. Vulnerability (VUL)/operating window **(T-3)**

2.2.4.6. Deconfliction plan (if applicable) **(T-3)**

2.2.4.7. Abort criteria and contingency plan **(T-3)**

2.2.4.8. Weapon system health/status **(T-3)**

2.2.5. The SQ/CC will ensure other activities, such as recurring academic training, training device periods, additional duties, etc., do not interfere with time allotted for mission planning and crew mission briefing/debriefing. **(T-3)**

2.2.6. Sortie. For planning purposes, the typical sortie duration is eight (8) hours.

## 2.3. Briefings.

2.3.1. The Crew Commander is responsible for presenting a logical briefing to promote a safe and effective mission(s) IAW local guidance. All crewmembers will attend the mission brief unless previously coordinated with squadron director of operations (SQ/DO).  **(T-3)**

2.3.2. The Crew Commander will plan adequate time to discuss required briefing items commensurate with the complexity of the mission and operator capabilities. **(T-3)**

2.3.2.1. Any item published in MAJCOM/Numbered Air Force (NAF)/wing/group/squadron standards or AFIs and understood by all participants may be briefed as "standard." **(T-3).**

2.3.3. Briefings will conclude no later than 15 minutes prior to scheduled sortie. **(T-3)**

2.3.4. Briefing Guides.  Briefing guides will be used by the lead briefer with a reference list of items which may apply to specific missions. Items may be briefed in any logical sequence; provided all minimum requirements listed in this AFI and other local directives and guidance are addressed. Refer to example briefing guide in Attachment 2. **(T-3).**

2.3.5. Crew members not attending the mission brief will receive, at a minimum, an overview of the mission objectives, their roles and responsibilities, current Crew Information File (CIF) read file and emergency procedures (EP) prior to beginning the mission.  This briefing will be accomplished by the Crew Commander **(T-3).**

2.3.6. Changed Mission Procedure.  A second mission brief will be conducted if the original plan and mission is cancelled, aborted, contingencies occur, or the mission was no-go for unplanned reasons (i.e., equipment malfunction, equipment availability, roles, etc.). The mission will be reviewed for differences and re-briefed for any changes (i.e., new deconfliction events to consider, different personnel executing the mission, VUL window, etc.). **(T-3)**

2.3.6.1. Mission deviations may occur during execution as long as they are briefed and mission safety is not compromised. The Crew Commander will ensure changes are acknowledged by all crewmembers. **(T-3)**

2.3.6.2. All mission deviations will be approved by the Crew Commander, or, if required, by a higher level authority. **(T-3)**

**Chapter 3**

**NORMAL OPERATING PROCEDURES**

**3.1. Pre-Mission Arrival Times.** The SQ/DO may adjust crew report time to meet mission requirements. Crew report times will allow sufficient time to accomplish all pre-mission activities. **(T-3)**

3.1.1. Scheduled vs Unscheduled. Crews will only be scheduled for duties related to the assigned sortie at least one (1) hour (scheduled) or four (4) hours (unscheduled) prior to the scheduled mission execution and regardless of duty day. If inadequate number of qualified personnel are on shift to perform mission planning, alternate crew members will be recalled or mission delay will be requested. **(T-3)**

3.1.2. Mission Planning Cell (MPC).  The MPC, when employed, will schedule and coordinate mission planning and disseminate all mission plans. The MPC will consist of a dedicated planning team, be responsible for Higher Headquarters (HHQ) taskings, assist with large force employment, and operational related squadron tasks. If an MPC is utilized, the SQ/DO or MPC Chief (MPCC) will establish the crew show time. **(T-3)**

**3.2. Crew Information File (CIF).** Crew members will review CIF for any new or revised information. This review will be conducted before all sorties and documented for record. Delinquent crew members will receive a CIF update from primary crew member counterparts prior to joining an ongoing sortie. **(T-3)**

**3.3. Go/No-Go.** The SQ/CC will implement the Go/No-Go program to ensure individual crew members are current, qualified, and/or adequately supervised to perform operations. Crew members will not operate on the weapon system until the Go/No-Go has been accomplished and verified. **(T-3)**

3.3.1. The SQ/CC will designate a crewmember, to conduct Go/No-Go verifications for a given VUL window. **(T-3)**

3.3.2. Designated individuals will verify, document, and sign off on the Go/No-Go status prior to releasing crew members for any scheduled missions. Go/No-Go accomplishment will be in the mission pre-brief as an essential briefing item. Records of the Go/No-Go accomplishment and verification will be maintained by the unit for one year in the station log. **(T-3)**

3.3.3. If automated functionality exists to accomplish the Go/No-Go verification, unit operating instructions will include backup procedures to permit Go/No-Go verification when the relevant information system is unavailable. **(T-3)**

3.3.4. The unit Go/No-Go process will verify the following for all crew members, to include instructors and evaluators, scheduled to perform crew duties.

3.3.4.1. Go/No-Go process will ensure qualification/certification of each scheduled crew member IAW AFI 17-2.AFINCV1, *Air Force Intranet Network Control (AFINC) Training* and AFI 17-2AFINCV2, *Air Force Intranet Control (AFNIC) Standardization and Evaluation. Note: Crewmembers not certified or in training status will require instructor or evaluator supervision to conduct crew duties.* **(T-3)**

3.3.4.2. Go/No-Go process will ensure currency and proficiency of each scheduled crew member IAW AFI 17-2.AFINCV1. *Note: Crewmembers not current in the crew position and/or mission will require instructor supervision to conduct crew duties until regaining currency.* **(T-3)**

3.3.4.3. Go/No-Go process will ensure each crew member reviews all CIF Read File items prior to conducting crew duties. **(T-3)**

**3.4. Unit-Developed Checklist/Local Crew Aids. (T-3)**

3.4.1. Locally developed checklists and crew aids shall be used and will, at a minimum, include the following:

3.4.1.1. Emergency action checklists and communication-out information. **(T-3)**

3.4.1.2. Other information as deemed necessary by the units. **(T-3)**

**3.5. Forms and Station Log.** The master station log is the unit's official record of events that occurred during operations or training. The log is intended to maintain an accurate and detailed record of all significant events pertaining to operations occurring during each sortie. All crew members are accountable for documenting significant events/crew actions required for the master station log. **(T-3)**

3.5.1. Crew members are responsible for content, accuracy, and timeliness of all inputs to mission-related information management portals/collaborative information sharing environments IAW applicable directives, tasking, and policy. **(T-3)**

**3.6. Required Publications.** All crew members will have all equipment and publications required for mission execution. These may be maintained and carried electronically, provided operable viewing and printing capability exists throughout mission execution. Standardization and Evaluation will maintain the list of required publication items in the CIF library. **(T-3)**

**3.7. Operations Check (Ops Check).** The Crew Commander is accountable for and will ensure required ops checks are accomplished to ensure safe and effective mission accomplishment(s). **(T-3)**

3.7.1. Crew Commander will ensure Ops Checks are conducted at initial check-in and prior to execution of missions. Crewmembers should check-in as soon as possible; after arrival and pre-checks are completed (i.e. on-station). Crew Commander will perform a roll-call directly before mission execution to ensure all teams are in place. **(T-3)**

**3.8. Abort/Knock-it-off.** A mission commander or Crew Commander may declare a knock-it-off (training use only) or abort (cease action/event/mission), if necessary.

**3.9. Dynamic Targeting.** During sorties, an operator may identify and report to HHQ potential targets and/or indicators that may require dynamic targeting. Dynamic targeting is executed during current operations against unplanned or unanticipated targets. HHQ can re-direct forces to engage the dynamic target. When engaging a dynamic target, the crew will follow the find, fix, track, target and engage and assess (F2T2EA) model. **(T-3)**

3.9.1. Crews will follow HHQ procedures to execute dynamic targeting. All dynamic targets must have HHQ approval prior to prosecution. **(T-2)**

3.9.2. Crews will document the new target/target request in the appropriate logs. **(T-3)**

**3.10. Dynamic Tasking.** During sorties, crews may identify and report situations that may require tasking to HHQ and tactical C2. Dynamic tasking allows for queuing of tasks into a mission to complete objectives in a changing battlespace. This includes everything from retasking an operator executing a mission to activating an entirely new on-call mission. Retasking is done through the tasking authority.

3.10.1. Crews will follow HHQ procedures to recommend dynamic tasking(s). Crew Commander/senior member will identify the mission that the task will be queued into using prescribed C2 channels. **(T-3)**

3.10.2. All dynamic task requests/recommendations must have HHQ approval prior to execution. **(T-2)**

3.10.3. Crews will document the retasking requirement in the appropriate logs and notify the mission planners. **(T-3)**

**3.11. Communications and Crew Coordination.** Recorded crew communications represent official communications.

3.11.1. Advisory Calls. The operator performing the execution will periodically announce their intentions during the critical checkpoints/phases of operations and when circumstances require deviating from normal procedures. **(T-3)**

3.11.2. Crews will use brevity codes defined in the Special Instructions (SPINS), applicable playbooks, and/or tactical mission planning to the maximum extent possible when conducting missions and making leadership notifications. **(T-3)**

3.11.3. Communications. Mission execution requires at least one method of communication for all operations. **(T-3)**

3.11.3.1. The mission planners are responsible for identifying any deviation from standard communication plan. **(T-3)**

**3.12. Mission Report (MISREP).** Crew Commander is responsible for providing timely, accurate, and correctly formatted reports to tasking authority. **(T-3)**

3.12.1. Tasking authorities, future missions and debriefs rely on accurate MISREPs in a timely manner. **(T-3)**

3.12.2. A MISREP will be accomplished once the crew has completed a mission or particular phase of the mission IAW guidance/tasking. **(T-3)**

3.12.3. Each crew member is responsible for providing the appropriate data regarding their mission area for the MISREP. **(T-3)**

3.12.4. Local procedures/templates may be developed to ensure standardization of reporting.

**3.13. Crew Changeover.** Crew members from the off-going and on-coming shifts will participate in a crew changeover briefing. At a minimum, the changeover will include a debrief on all completed actions and a current situation report on ongoing activity. **(T-3)**

**3.14. Positional Changeover Brief.** Crews are required to brief oncoming crewmembers. A positional changeover briefing with the oncoming crewmember will be delivered IAW checklist(s) and applicable directives. The changeover brief will include, but is not limited to, plans associated with upcoming missions, lessons learned from previous crew changeover debriefs, in addition to interim updates to processes or procedures. **(T-3)**

**3.15. Debriefing.**

3.15.1. The Crew Commander /senior crew member will lead a thorough mission debrief for every sortie. **(T-3)**

3.15.2. Debriefs will cover all aspects of the planning, briefing and execution of every sortie, or event (as needed), IAW local guidance. **(T-3)**

3.15.3. Crew Commander is responsible for assessing crew effectiveness.

3.15.4. Debriefs will be conducted at all levels of execution. **(T-3)**

**3.16. Post Sortie Duties.**

3.16.1. Crews will document all completed CT, on appropriate training accomplishment reports and submit IAW unit guidance. **(T-3)**

# Chapter 4

## CREW DUTIES, RESPONSIBILITIES, AND PROCEDURES

**4.1. AFINC Responsibilities.** The Crew Commander is responsible for all aspects of the safe operation of the AFINC weapon system. Mission crew manning may vary by the type of mission. There must be a Crew Commander, Ops Controller, Operator(s) and at least one SMQ operator, as required, per functional area on-station during a sortie. SQ/CC or SQ/DO may tailor crew manning to meet operational requirements. If an event occurs that causes the AFINC to change to its Alternate Operating Location (AOL) mission responsibility will only transfer if there are qualified personnel to fill the minimum crew positions (i.e. a Crew Commander, an Ops Controller and operators). In most cases, mission responsibility will remain with the Crew Commander at the Primary Operating Location (POL). **(T-3)**

**4.2. Crew Stations.** Crew members shall be in their assigned crew duty position during the critical checkpoints/phases of execution. Crew members will notify the Crew Commander prior to departing their assigned crew duty position. **(T-3)**

**4.3. Crew Duties.** Crew members are responsible for successful sortie/mission execution. Crew members are responsible for the safe, effective use of the weapon system.

**4.4. Crew Positions.** The following crew positions must maintain certification/qualification status IAW AFI 17-202V2, *Cybercrew Standardization and Evaluation Program.*

4.4.1. AFINC Crew Commander.  Serves as the command authority for AFINC crew operations and provides command oversight for crew members as well as enforcing policies and procedures to ensure successful mission accomplishment. The Crew Commander is the liaison between the Cyber Crew and AFINC leadership and other outside agencies. **(T-3)**

4.4.1.1. The Crew Commander will manage crew resources for safe mission accomplishment. **(T-3)**

4.4.1.2. The Crew Commander will ensure any portion of the operation affecting the accomplishment of the mission is coordinated with the tasking authority. The Crew Commander will ensure risk management decision matrix is performed prior to leading mission planning, pre-mission brief, mission execution, post-mission activities and debrief. **(T-3)**

4.4.2. AFINC Operations Controller.  The Ops controller is responsible for management of the operator's execution of assigned missions/sorties. Multiple ops controllers can be assigned to a crew to manage multiple sorties. **(T-3)**

4.4.3. Air Force Intranet Control Basic Operator (AFINC-O).  Employs the weapon system in the conduct of surveillance and reconnaissance activities. **(T-3)**

4.4.4. Crew Operator Special Mission Qualifications

4.4.4.1. Domain Name Server/Email Gateway Operator (DNS/Email Gateway Operator). Coordinates defensive maneuvers for Air Force-level DNS and email. Provides analysis of traffic originating from/to AF domains and sub-domains. The DNS/Email Gateway operator will collect traffic to allow for threat detection, countermeasure development and deployment, forensic analysis, and current TTP employment. DNS/Email Gateway operator will perform defensive maneuvers under the direction of the Crew Commander/senior crewmembers. **(T-3)**

4.4.4.2. Router Operator. Defends the Air Force Wide Area Networks, service delivery point (SDP) router fleet, and the AF Common User VPN. The Router operator will perform defensive maneuvers under the direction of the Crew Commander/Ops Controller. **(T-3)**

4.4.4.3. Boundary Protection Operator. Defends the Air Force Wide Area Networks, Global Command and Control System (GCCS) utilizing firewalls and web proxies. The Boundary Protection Operator will perform defensive maneuvers under the direction of the Crew Commander/senior crew members. **(T-3)**

4.4.4.4. AFINC Analyst. Provides specialized threat analysis and detection spanning across multiple platforms throughout the AFINC weapons system. Develops countermeasures and defensive maneuvers to continuously shape and defend the Air Force Wide Area Networks. Coordinates with intelligence cells to evaluate threats and corresponding TTPs. AFINC Analyst is not a crew positions, but is a back shop function. **(T-3)**

**4.5. Crew Qualification.** Each person assigned as a primary crewmember will be current and qualified or in a training status under the supervision of a qualified instructor in that crew position and mission. **(T-3)**

4.5.1. Basic cyber crew qualified (BCQ) crewmembers may perform primary crew duties when receiving MQT or evaluations under the supervision of a qualified instructor/evaluator in their respective crew position.

4.5.2. Basic mission capable (BMC) crewmembers may perform primary crew duties on any operational mission when teamed with an MR crewmember. The SQ/CC must determine the readiness of each BMC crewmember to perform primary crew duties. **(T-3)**

4.5.3. Mission ready (MR) crewmembers may perform primary crew duties in any position in which they maintain qualification, certification, currency and proficiency.

4.5.4. Non-current or unqualified crew may perform crew duties only on designated training or evaluation missions under the supervision of a qualified instructor, evaluator.

4.5.5. Unless waived by the SQ CC/DO, unqualified crew members will perform operations with a certified instructor in the same position at all times, until certified. **(T-3)**

**4.6. New/Modified Equipment and/or Capabilities.** Crew members not qualified and/or certified in the operation of new or modified equipment and/or weapon system capabilities will not operate that equipment or perform any duties associated with that weapon system capability(ies) unless under the supervision of a current and qualified instructor . **(T-3)**

**4.7. Crew Rest/Duty Period/Sortie Duration.** Crew rest, crew duty period and crew augmentation will be IAW AFI 17-202V3 and all applicable guidance with the following additional guidance:

4.7.1. Crew Rest. Commanders will ensure crews are afforded a minimum 12-hour non-duty crew rest before the duty period begins to ensure the crew member receives an opportunity for rest before performing a mission or mission-related duties. Crew rest is free time, and includes time for meals, transportation and 8 hours of uninterrupted rest. Rest is defined as a condition that allows an individual the opportunity to sleep. Each crew member is individually responsible for ensuring they obtain sufficient rest during crew rest periods. **(T-3)**

4.7.2. Exceptions to the 12-Hour Minimum Crew Rest Period. For continuous operations when basic crew duty periods are greater than 12 but less than 14 hours, subsequent crew rest may be reduced proportionally to a minimum of 10 hours with OG/CC approval. **(T-3)**

4.7.2.1. Continuous operations mean three or more consecutive sorties of at least 12 hours duration separated by minimum crew rest. **(T-3)**

4.7.2.2. The crew rest exception shall only be used for contingency/surge operations and not for scheduling conveniences. **(T-3)**

4.7.3. Duty Period. The normal crew duty period is eight (8) hours with a maximum of twelve (12) hours which includes planning, briefing and debriefing. **(T-3)**

**4.8. Crew Scheduling.** Scheduling mission crews will be accomplished IAW crew rest limitations provided in this AFI.

4.8.1. Units will attempt to provide all crew members as stable a schedule as possible. **(T-3)**

4.8.2. Units are responsible to publish, post, and monitor schedules for the crew force and initiate changes to the schedules based on proper tracking of qualifications, certifications, restrictions and other factors required to meet mission objectives. **(T-3)**

4.8.2.1. Commanders will ensure a crew member on leave or temporary duty (TDY) is notified if a schedule change places or changes an event on their schedule no later than the first 72 hours of their scheduled return. **(T-3)**

4.8.2.2. Notifications will be made as soon as practical after the change is official, but not later than 24 hours prior to the scheduled event time. Units will ensure that oncoming crewmembers are capable of meeting crew risk management requirements in addition to ensuring that crewmembers are not under the effects of alcohol within 12 hours prior to mission planning/execution. **(T-3)**

WILLIAM J. BENDER, Lt Gen, USAF
Chief of Information Dominance and
Chief Information Officer

**Attachment 1**

**GLOSSARY OF REFERENCES AND SUPPORTING INFORMATION**

*References*

AFPD 17-2, *Cyberspace Operations,* 12 April 2016

AFI 17-202 Vol 1, *Cybercrew Training,* 2 Apr 2014

AFI 17-202 Vol 2, *Cybercrew Standardization and Evaluation Program,* 15 October 2014

AFI 17-202 Vol 3, *Cyberspace Operations and Procedures,* 6 May 2015

AFI 17-2AFINCV1, *Air Force Intranet Network Control (AFNIC) Training*

AFI 17-2AFINCV2, *Air Force Intranet Control (AFNIC) Standardization and Evaluation*

AFI 33-360, *Publications and Forms Management,* 1 December 2015

AFMAN 33-363, *Management of Records,* 1 March 2008, (*Incorporating Change* 2, 9 June 2016, *Certified Current* 21 July 2016)

AFI 11-215, *USAF Mission Manuals Program (FMP),* 22 Dec 2008 (IC1, 28 Oct 2010, *Certified Current* 3 Jan 2011)

AFTTP 3-1.AFINC

AFCYBER & JFHQ-C AFCYBER Tactical Mission Planning, Briefing and Debriefing Guide

AFTTP 3-1.General Planning

AFTTP 3-1.Threat Guide **Chapter 13**

USAFWS "A MC's Handbook," Captain Brad J. Bashore, 13 Dec 2008

USAFWS "ME3C-(PC)2: A Problem Solving Methodology," Captain Raymond L. Daniel, 13 June 2009

USAFWS "Methodology of the Debrief," Captain Robert L. Brown, 10 June 2006

MULTI-SERVICE BREVITY CODES, AFTTP 3-2.5, September 2014

FB 12-12, Defensive Cyberspace Operations-Tactical Coordinator

FB 14-19 Defensive Cyber Operations Large Force Employment Considerations

*Adopted Forms*

AF Form 679, *Air Force Publication Compliance Item Waiver Request/Approval*

AF Form 847, *Recommendation for Change of Publication*

AFTO Form 781, *ARMS Crew/Mission Flight Data Document*

*Abbreviations and Acronyms*

**AF**—Air Force

**AFI**—Air Force Instruction

**AFCYBER**—Air Force Cyber Command

**AFPD**—Air Force Policy Directive

**AFINC**—Air Force Intranet Control

**AFINC/CC**—Air Force Intranet Control Crew Commander

**AFMAN**—Air Force Manual

**AFRC**—Air Force Reserve Command

**AFRDS**—Air Force Records Disposition Schedule

**AFRIMS**—Air Force Records Information Management System

**AFSPC**—Air Force Space Command

**AFTTP**—Air Force Tactics, Techniques and Procedures

**ANG**—Air National Guard

**AOL**—Alternate Operating Location

**ASD**—Average Sortie Duration

**BCQ**—Basic Cybercrew Qualification

**BMC**—Basic Mission Capable

**CB**—Crew Bulletin

**CC**—Commander

**AFINC/CC**—AFINC Crew Commander

**CIF**—Crew Information File

**AFINC/OC**—AFINC Operations Controller

**CT**—Continuation Training

**DO**—Director of Operations

**DV**—Distinguished Visitor

**EP**—Emergency Procedures

**GTIMS**—Graduate Training Integration Management System

**HHQ**—Higher Headquarters

**IAW**—In Accordance With

**JFHQ-C** – Joint Forces Headquarters-Cyber

**LL**—Lesson Learned

**LP**—Learning Point

**MAJCOM**—Major Command

**MISREP**—Mission Report

**MPC**—Mission Planning Cell

**MPT**—Mission Planning Team

**MR**—Mission Ready

**NAF**—Numbered Air Force

**OG**—Operations Group

**OGV**—Standardization and Evaluation

**Ops Check**—Operations Check

**OPR**—Office of Primary Responsibility

**POL**—Primary Operating Location

**ROE**—Rules of Engagement

**SOP**—Standard Operating Procedures

**SPINS**—Special Instructions

**SQ**—Squadron

**TOT/T**—Time over Target/Terrain

**USAF**—United States Air Force

**VUL**—Vulnerability

*Terms*

**Air Force Intranet Control Operator (AFINC/O)**— Operates the AFINC Alert mission conducting enduring enterprise-wide, friendly and adversary force monitoring, and alerting for the intended purpose of nominating targets for further action (i.e., intercepting and mitigating malicious adversaries/activity).

**Average Sortie Duration (ASD)**— ASD is used to convert sorties to execution hours and vice versa. MAJCOM/A3TB uses the unit's last programmed ASD when initially determining execution hour's programs for the current and future years. Units will update ASD annually to reflect the unit's best estimate of the optimum sortie duration after considering historical experiences, changes in missions, deployments, etc. The formula to calculate ASD is ASD=# of weapon system hours employed divided by number of sorties.

**Basic Mission Capable (BMC)**— The status of a crewmember who satisfactorily completed IQT and MQT to perform the unit's basic operational missions, but does not maintain MR/CMR proficiency. Crewmember accomplishes training required to remain familiarized in all and may be qualified and proficient in some of the primary missions of their weapon system BMC requirements. These crewmembers may also maintain special mission qualification.

**Basic Cybercrew Qualification (BCQ)**— A cybercrew member who satisfactorily completed IQT. The crewmember will carry BCQ only until completion of MQT. BCQ crewmembers will not perform RCP-tasked events or sorties without instructor crewmembers.

**Certification**— Designation of an individual by the certifying official as having completed required training and/or evaluation and being capable of performing a specific duty.

**Continuation Training (CT)**— Training which provides crew members with the volume, frequency, and mix of training necessary to maintain currency and proficiency in the assigned qualification level.

**Crew Commander**— Responsible for AFINC crew operations and provides command oversight for operations floor personnel. Enforces compliance with policies and procedures to ensure successful mission accomplishment.

**Crew Information File (CIF)**— A collection of publications and material identified by the MAJCOM and unit as necessary for day-to-day operations.

**Crew**— Consists of a Crew Commander, Ops Controller and operators.

**Currency**— A measure of how frequently and/or recently a task is completed. Currency requirements should ensure the average crew member maintains a minimum level of proficiency in a specific event.

**Cyberspace Operations (CO)**— The employment of cyberspace capabilities where the primary purpose is to achieve objectives in or through cyberspace.

**Deviation**— Performing action(s) not in compliance with current procedures, directives, or regulations. Performing action(s) not in compliance due to unusual or extenuating circumstances is not considered a deviation. In some cases, momentary deviations may be acceptable; however, cumulative deviations will be considered in determining the overall qualification level.

**Mission**— Missions are operations conducted with an intended purpose. Missions are conducted by a unit and/or units with relevant capability and preponderance of capacity. The base mechanism used to achieve mission objectives are sorties. Missions may require multiple sorties from multiple units to accomplish the mission objectives.

**Mission Ready (MR)**— A crew member who satisfactorily completed IQT and MQT, and maintains certification, currency and proficiency in the command or unit mission.

**Non-current (NC) or Unqualified (UNQ)**—crew may perform crew duties only on designated training or evaluation missions under the supervision of a qualified instructor/examiner.

**Qualification**— Designation of an individual by the SQ/CC as having completed required training and evaluation and being capable of performing a specific duty.

**Sortie**— The actions an individual weapon system takes to accomplish a mission and/or mission objective(s) within a defined start and stop period.

**Target**— The adversary, purposeful malicious actor code, or processes residing in blue or gray terrain. Targets include, but are not limited to, processes, code, credentials, storage, and the countering of adversary tactics, techniques and procedures designed to establish persistent access and C2.

**Task**— A clearly defined action or activity specifically assigned to an individual or organization that must be accomplished as it is imposed by an appropriate authority.

**Terrain**— The cyberspace area of operations where a force package is directed to conduct a sortie. Terrain is defined as Internet Protocol (IP) address, domain, or transport space within the DoDIN or AF enclave (commonly referred to as "blue" space), or commercial, contractor-owned mission partner-owned ("grey" space) host, server, and network devices that enable C2, communication, sensing, and access capabilities.

**Time Over Target/Terrain (TOT)**— The exact timing requested by the tactical commander, directed by the tasking authority, or specified in the tasking order to prosecute a mission. The TOT is based on the available Vulnerability (VUL) window (can be an enduring or time-sensitive requirement) and must be executed within the vul window; authorization for a TOT outside a vul window can only be authorized by the tasking authority.

**Vulnerability (VUL) Window**— his is a window of opportunity and direction for a tactical commander to conduct operations. A VUL Window is bounded (start by/finish by) to give a tactical commander the authorized and suspensed timing available to plan and prosecute mission. Deviations from the assigned VUL Window must be approved by the tasking authority.

Weapon System - A combination of one or more weapons with all related equipment, materials, services, personnel, and means of delivery and deployment (if applicable) required for self-sufficiency.

*BY ORDER OF THE*
*SECRETARY OF THE AIR FORCE*

*AIR FORCE INSTRUCTION 33-115*

*16 SEPTEMBER 2014*

*Incorporating Change 1, 15 September 2016*

*Communications and Information*

*AIR FORCE INFORMATION TECHNOLOGY
(IT) SERVICE MANAGEMENT*

**COMPLIANCE WITH THIS PUBLICATION IS MANDATORY**

**ACCESSIBILITY:** Publications and forms are available for downloading or ordering on the e-Publishing website at **http://www.e-publishing.af.mil.**

**RELEASABILITY:** There are no releasability restrictions on this publication.

---

OPR: SAF/CIO A6SE

Certified by: SAF/CIO A6S
(Brig Gen Patrick C. Higby)
Pages: 56

Supersedes: AFI33-115V1, 24 May 2006
AFI33-115V2, 14 April 2004
AFI33-115 V3, 15 April 2004
AFI33-129, 3 February 2005
AFI33-138, 28 November 2005

---

This Air Force Instruction (AFI) defines AF IT Service Management and assigns responsibilities for standardization and management of IT Services in the AF. This instruction implements AF Policy Directive (AFPD) 33-1, *Cyberspace Support,* Department of Defense (DoD) Instruction (DoDI) 8410.01, *Internet Domain Name Use and Approval,* DoDI 8410.02, *NetOps for the Global Information Grid (GIG),* DoDI 8410.03, *Network Management (NM)* and DoDI 8550.01, *DoD Internet Services and Internet-Based Capabilities.* This instruction is consistent with AFPD 33-2, *Information Assurance (IA) Program;* AFPD 33-3, *Information Management;* AFPD 33-4, *Information Technology Governance;* and AFPD 10-17, *Cyberspace Operations.* This instruction provides guidance, direction and assigns responsibilities for the Air Force Information Networks (AFIN) as the Air Force provisioned portion of the DoD Information Networks (DoDIN). This directive applies to all military and civilian Air Force personnel, the Air Force Reserve (AFR), and Air National Guard (ANG). This publication shall be applied to contractors or other persons through the contract or other legally binding agreement with the Department of the Air Force. The authorities to waive wing/unit level requirements in this publication are identified with a Tier ("T-0, T-1, T-2, T-3") number following the compliance statement. See AFI 33-360, *Publications and Forms Management,* Table 1.1 for a description of the authorities associated with the Tier numbers. Submit requests for waivers through the chain of command to the appropriate Tier waiver approval authority, or alternately, to the Publication OPR for non-tiered compliance items. Send recommended changes or comments to the Air

Force Cyberspace Strategy & Policy Division (SAF/A6CS) using AF Form 847, *Recommendation for Change of Publication.*

Ensure that all records created as a result of processes prescribed in this publication are maintained in accordance with (IAW) Air Force Manual (AFMAN) 33-363, *Management of Records*, and disposed of in accordance with Air Force Records Information Management System (AFRIMS) Records Disposition Schedule (RDS). See **Attachment 1** for a glossary of references and supporting information.

## *SUMMARY OF CHANGES*

This interim change revises AFI 33-115 by (1) incorporating cloud computing and storage guidance (2) removing references to DISA as the cloud broker throughout the document (3) including other hosting infrastructure types and (4) incorporating the AFGM from 29 Oct 2015. A margin bar (|) indicates changed material.

| | | |
|---|---|---|
| 1. | Purpose. | 3 |
| 2. | Objectives. | 3 |
| 3. | Background. | 3 |
| Figure 1. | Information Environment Relationships. | 4 |
| 4. | Roles and Responsibilities. | 5 |
| 5. | AF IT Services Framework. | 21 |
| Figure 2. | AF IT Services Framework. | 21 |
| Figure 3. | Air Force Application Rationalization Process. | 30 |
| Figure 4. | Air Force Application Migration Execution Framework. | 31 |
| Figure 5. | Air Force Application Migration Process Flowchart (DISCOVERY). | 32 |
| Figure 5.1. | Air Force Application Migration Process Flowchart (ASSESSMENT & ANALYSIS). | 33 |
| Figure 5.2. | Air Force Application Migration Process Flowchart (CONDUCT PLANNING). | 34 |
| Figure 5.3. | Air Force Application Migration Process Flowchart (MIGRATE APPLICATION). | 35 |
| 6. | AFIN Baseline Management. | 37 |
| Figure 6. | HAF/SAF IT/Cyberspace Operational Baseline Modification Process. | 38 |
| 7. | Operation of AF IT Services within the AFIN. | 39 |
| **Attachment 1—GLOSSARY OF REFERENCES AND SUPPORTING INFORMATION** | | **45** |

**1. Purpose.** This instruction defines AF IT Service Management and assigns responsibilities for the configuration, provisioning, maintenance, and management of AFIN using an IT Service Management (ITSM) framework to further integrate capabilities and maintain configuration control of AF networks and data servers.  This instruction serves as the single reference for AF IT Service Management policy and applies to all personnel who manage, configure, operate, maintain, defend, or extend any portion of the AFIN or provide support within the AF for the DoDIN and the Joint Information Environment (JIE).

1.1. Procedural guidance supporting this AFI is contained in Methods and Procedures Technical Orders (MPTOs) directing standard processes for management, standardization, and maintenance of AF IT Services applicable to all AF personnel, see **paragraph 7.3**.

1.2. Cyberspace operational orders as defined in AFI 10-1701 (e.g., AF Cyber Tasking Orders, Cyber Control Orders, AF Time Compliance Network Orders) shall take precedence over information contained in this AFI and supporting MPTOs if there is a conflict.

**2. Objectives.** The primary objective of this AFI is to establish and define AF IT Service Management  with roles and responsibilities to ensure the AFIN is designed, built, configured, secured, operated, maintained, and sustained to meet mission requirements.  This AFI also provides guidance regarding migration of AF enterprise capabilities (core services, applications, and systems) to the JIE according to DoD guidance.  AF IT Service Management integrates, secures, and manages the AFNET/AFNET-S with processes and capabilities to enable the seamless, secure, and reliable exchange of information across the AFIN and the DoDIN.  The AFNET is the AF's underlying unclassified network that enables AF operational capabilities and lines of business.  AFNET-S is the secure AFNET.

2.1. This AFI and supporting 00-33 series MPTOs shall not alter or supersede the existing authorities and policies of the Director of National Intelligence (DNI) regarding the protection of Sensitive Compartmented Information (SCI) systems or intelligence, surveillance, reconnaissance mission and mission support systems or higher authoritative guidance governing Special Access Program (SAP) systems.  When DNI or SAP authorities fail to address areas covered by this AFI, this AFI and associated MPTOs will be followed.  If there is conflict between this AFI and associated MPTOs with guidance issued by DNI or SAP authorities, DNI or SAP guidance will take precedence.

2.2. For this instruction, the term Major Command (MAJCOM) also applies to Numbered Air Force (NAF), Field Operating Agency (FOA) and Direct Reporting Unit (DRU) when not assigned to a MAJCOM.

2.3. All AF organizations will follow this policy when extending AF IT Services.

**3. Background.** The AF Information Environment consists of AF unique information capabilities across the IT Governance Mission Areas: Business (BMA), Warfighting (WMA), Defense Intelligence (DIMA) and Information Environment (IEMA).  The AF Information Environment includes the IT systems, components and networks of the Defense Business Systems, National Security Systems (NSS), Platform IT, Enterprise Core Services and Common Computing Environments as depicted in **Figure 1**.  The AFIN is the globally interconnected, end-to-end set of AF unique information capabilities and associated processes for collecting, processing, storing, disseminating, and managing information on-demand to warfighters, policy makers, and support personnel, including owned and leased communications and computing systems and services, software (including applications), data, and security.   The AFIN can be considered the networked AF Information Environment.  Where known, this AFI will depict the specific AF capabilities and services which will transition to DoD's secure joint information environment (JIE).  JIE is comprised of shared IT infrastructure, enterprise services, and a single security architecture to achieve full spectrum superiority, improve mission effectiveness, increase security and realize IT efficiencies.

**Figure 1.  Information Environment Relationships.**

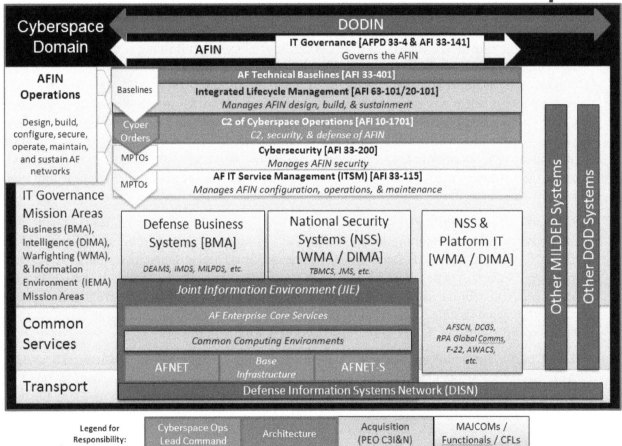

3.1. AF IT Service Management enables a robust and resilient net-centric environment providing the means to establish and extend the AFIN.  AF IT Service Management supports rapidly evolving mission processes and warfighter requirements which require an optimized, stable, and enterprise managed AFIN postured to integrate with and support the JIE.  AF IT Service Management encompasses management of common IT functions, actions, and capabilities to provide Common Computing Environments, Application Support Services, and Enterprise Core Services. Additionally, AF ITSM standardizes select ITSM processes for all information systems (e.g., Vulnerability Management).

3.2. AF IT Service Management is aligned with the Defense Information Technology Infrastructure Library (ITIL) as it transitions to the Defense Enterprise Service Management Framework (DESMF), and DoD Directive (DoDD) 8000.01, *Management of the Department of Defense Information Enterprise*. These services and the standard methods and procedures in the supporting MPTOs will continue to evolve to support the AF's management of IT under the JIE construct. These services must align with high level guidance and strategic goals of the AF Enterprise Architecture. For more information on enterprise architecture, see AFI 33-401, *Air Force Architecting*.

3.3. AFI 10-1701 implements the C2 of Cyberspace Operations and while this AFI directs specific ITSM functions which support DoDIN Operations. Together, these two instructions direct operations and support of the AFIN for the business and warfighting mission areas including the Cyberspace Operations mission. Capabilities to secure and protect the AFIN must be integrated throughout AF networks and systems following Cybersecurity policy (previously known as IA). Cybersecurity inherent in AF networks and systems are further enhanced by Defensive Cyberspace Operations (DCO) under Cyberspace Operations. DCO may be integrated with or direct changes to cybersecurity in AF networks and systems under C2 of Cyberspace Operations as it directs AFIN operations and defense. Note: DoD defines DoDIN Operations as the actions taken to design, build, configure, secure, operate, maintain, and sustain DOD communications systems and networks in a way that creates and preserves data availability, integrity, confidentiality, as well as user/entity authentication and non-repudiation.

**4. Roles and Responsibilities.** Roles and responsibilities for AF IT Service Management are a coordinated effort between all organizations providing, supporting, and utilizing IT in the AFIN, the DoDIN, and the JIE. AF functional communities or DoD organizations such as Defense Information Systems Agency (DISA) or AFSPC will have primary or supporting roles when AF IT Services are consolidated at the DoD-enterprise level and JIE. Roles and responsibilities for C2 of Cyberspace within AFI 10-1701 provides clear command and control over these collaborative relationships and is to be used in conjunction with this AFI.

4.1. **Chief, Information Dominance and Chief Information Officer (SAF/CIO A6).** SAF/CIO A6 has overall responsibility for the AFIN, information technology (IT), IT Service Management responsibilities for National Security Systems (NSS), defense business systems, and information resource management matters according to AFPD 33-1. SAF/CIO A6 will:

4.1.1. Provide strategy, policy, guidance, and oversight for the AF portion of the DoD information enterprise, including communications, spectrum management, network management, information systems, and cybersecurity.

4.1.1.1. Develop AF strategy and policy on the operation and protection of all AF IT and information systems within the AFIN as the AF provisioned portion of the DoDIN, including development and promulgation of enterprise-wide architecture requirements and technical standards, and enforcement, operation, and maintenance of systems, interoperability, collaboration, and interface between AF and non-AF systems, and investment and cost effectiveness of information system acquisition and sustainment.

4.1.1.2. Maintain a consolidated inventory of AF mission-critical and mission-essential information systems, identify interfaces between these systems, and ensure the development and test of contingency plans for responding to disruptions in the operation of any of these information systems.

4.1.1.3. Provide guidance and oversight for AF network management, including the standards for day-to-day security and protection of AF information networks; AF IT support to joint missions; and resilience and reliability of information and communication networks.

4.1.1.4. Provide guidance and oversight on the administration of AF Internet services, use of Internet-based capabilities, and all Internet domain-related functions.

4.1.1.5. Develop strategy, policy, and guidance for AF use of private and public cloud computing services in support of the AFIN. Review DoD Cloud Computing Security Requirements Guide (SRG) for commercial cloud services and coordinate any modifications needed for alignment between the DoD cloud security model and the AFIN technical architecture security controls provided in the Target Baseline according to AFPD 33-4, Information Technology Governance.

4.1.2. Provide governance of IT according to AFPD 33-4, *Information Technology Governance*, including oversight for compliance with the Target Baseline (TB), Implementation Baseline (IB), and Operational Baseline (OB).

4.1.3. Define the AF IT Service Management for the AFIN and ensure Enterprise Core Services for the AF are in-line with the DoD Enterprise Services under the DoDIN and/or JIE.

4.1.4. Provide oversight of the implementation status of AF IT Services on behalf of the Secretary of the Air Force (SECAF) and Chief of Staff of the Air Force (CSAF).

4.1.5. Fulfill AF CIO responsibilities of DoDI 8550.01, *DoD Internet Services and Internet-Based Capabilities.*

4.1.6. Provide oversight and guidance for personnel development, career field management, and training of AF Cyberspace career fields according to AFI 36-2640, *Executing Total Force Development.*

4.1.7. Deleted.

4.1.8. Coordinate with Air Force Office of the Judge Advocate General (AF/JA), the Air Force Office of Special Investigations (AFOSI), the Air Force Office of the Inspector General (SAF/IG), the Intelligence Community, and the Acquisition Division of the Air Force General Counsel (SAF/GCQ) to provide sensitive information protection requirements.

4.1.9. Coordinate with Air Force Legal Operations Agency (AFLOA), SAF/GC, AF/JAA and SAF/AQC to provide requirements to Cloud Service Providers (CSPs) for compliance with AF e-Discovery, FOIA, and investigative purposes IAW with AFI-33-364, AFMAN 33-363, DOD5400.7-R_AFMAN33-302, and AFI 51-301.

4.1.10. Act as the approval authority for waiver requests to deviate from the requirements of this publication.

4.1.11. Act as the central AF approval authority for obligations to acquire servers, data centers, and IT technology therein, IAW AFI 33-150, *Management of Cyberspace Support Activities*, **Attachment 2**.

4.1.12. Establish procedures to ensure compliance with the Privacy Act and the DoD privacy program. Appoint a Component Senior Official for Privacy (CSOP) with overall responsibility for the AF privacy program. Appoint an AF Privacy Officer with responsibility for implementing the AF privacy program. Ensure that all systems that contains personal identifiable information have an up to data privacy impact assessment and if the data is contained in a system or record (SOR) has a current System of Records Notice (SORN) that accurately reflects the data being collected, the purpose of collecting the data, how/ to whom the data is released, and the location where the data is located (AFI 33-332).

4.2. **IT Governance Executive Board (ITGEB) will:**

4.2.1. Approve the data centers (Installation Processing Node [IPN], Installation Services Node [ISN], Special Purpose Processing Node [SPPN]) to serve as AF data center infrastructure. ITGEB-approved data centers are the only authorized data centers for the AF to employ application hosting and provisioning of private cloud services. See AFPD 33-4 for more information on the ITGEB.

4.2.2. Oversee the execution of application rationalization and migration across the AF to ensure compliance with DoD guidance regarding hosting within IPNs, Core Data Centers (CDCs), MilCloud, SPPNs, Tactical Processing Nodes (TPNs) and the commercial cloud environment. This includes directing the capture and reporting of metrics reflecting decommissioned servers and data centers in accordance with the Federal Data Center Consolidation Initiative (FDCCI).

4.2.3. The scope for the ITGEB includes the entire AF IT enterprise for business and mission capabilities, including business and national security systems (NSS), and excluding the embedded software in support of weapons platforms. This team shall focus on the commoditization and operational configuration management of a baseline IT infrastructure and the business practices to exploit that IT infrastructure for AF users. The details of membership and processes can be found in AFPD 33-4.

4.3. **Secretary of the Air Force Office of Public Affairs (SAF/PA) will:**

4.3.1. Develop guidance for the integration of public web sites into the Air Force Public Web Program. Serve as chair of the Air Force Public Web Policy Board.

4.3.2. Develop guidance governing the public communication program.

4.3.3. Review and approve/disapprove waiver requests for AF public Web sites hosted outside the scope of the Air Force Public Web Program.

4.4. **Assistant Secretary of the Air Force for Acquisition (SAF/AQ).** As the Senior Acquisition Executive, SAF/AQ will:

4.4.1. Oversee the acquisition and sustainment of capabilities that support the AFIN.

4.4.2. Work with SAF/CIO A6 and AFSPC to procure, develop, integrate and test the AFIN components and systems in accordance with the Implementation Baseline.

4.4.3. Collaborate with SAF/CIO A6 in developing the Implementation Baseline (IB) defined in AFPD 33-4. Ensure AF acquisition programs comply with the established IB requirements.

4.4.4. Ensure AF acquisition programs leverage, to the maximum extent possible, the use of JIE Enterprise Core Services, and promote sharing of data, information, and knowledge throughout the AF corporate structure.

4.4.5. Coordinate with SAF/CIO A6 to develop strategy, policy, and guidance to provide an AF enterprise approach for acquiring cloud computing services.

4.4.6. Ensure all Acquisition Category (ACAT) programs address the requirements of National Defense Authorization Act (NDAA) Fiscal Year 2012 Section 2867 and AFI 33-150, *Management of Cyberspace Support Activities*, **Attachment 2**, in the acquisition of servers, data centers, and IT technology.

**4.5. Air Force Material Command (AFMC).** As the Implementing Command defined by AFI 63-101/20-101, AFMC has overall responsibility for supporting the design, build, and sustainment of the AFIN. AFMC will:

4.5.1. In coordination with AFSPC, provide technical assistance to SAF/CIO A6 to develop policy and guidance for the AFIN.

4.5.2. Provide integration and test capability for IT components to support the development environment of new capabilities and troubleshooting performance issues with fielded capabilities, as required.

4.5.3. Provide direction and guidance to ensure all Program Executive Offices (PEOs) comply with the single AF approach for cloud computing and establish the AF Cloud Service Lead according to **paragraph 4.6.5.**

4.5.4. Oversee the work performed by PEO C3I&N on the commoditized infrastructure Implementation Baseline.

4.5.5. In coordination with AFSPC, oversee the deployment of all AF IT services.

4.5.6. Oversee the standup of the IT lifecycle integration and test capability.

**4.6. The Program Executive Office for Command, Control, Communications, Intelligence and Networks (PEO C3I&N).** PEO C3I&N will:

4.6.1. Perform Service Design and Development to include engineering, architecture, and provisioning support for AFNET, AFNET-S, and PEO C3I&N-provided systems within the AFIN and JIE in coordination with SAF/CIO A6 and AFSPC. Provides integration of AF IT across all systems centers (e.g., Air Force Life Cycle Management Center, Space and Missile Systems Center, Air Force Medical Support Agency, Air Force Nuclear Weapons Center).

4.6.2. Establish, publish, and maintain the commoditized infrastructure Implementation Baseline in accordance with AFPD 33-4.

4.6.3. Facilitate the standup and operation of an IT lifecycle integration and test capability supporting the development, test, and delivery of new warfighter capabilities utilizing the Implementation Baseline.  Leverage existing DoD, AF and Contractor resources to establish a virtual, distributed system development, integration and test capability supporting the delivery of new warfighter capabilities.

4.6.4. Support mission capabilities offices in configuring and provisioning the Implementation Baseline to meet requirements.  Support mission capabilities offices with transitioning their newly developed capabilities into the Implementation Baseline integration environment leading to deployment.

4.6.5. Managed Service Office (MSO) will serve as the lead for both the cloud and Application Rationalization and Migration Process:

4.6.5.1.  Review and validate all customer cloud computing requirements.

4.6.5.2.  Deleted.

4.6.6. Ensure a standardized AF process is adhered to for common computing environments and cloud services, including Infrastructure-as-a-Service (IaaS), Platform-as-a-Service (PaaS), and Software-as-a-Service (SaaS) as detailed in paragraph 5.3  Fully leverage DoD efforts to provide a DoD Enterprise Cloud Environment under the JIE in accordance with DoD CIO Memorandum, DoD Cloud Computing Strategy Memorandum, 5 July 2012 and DoD CIO Supplemental Guidance Memo, 15 December 2014.

4.6.6.1.  Review all AF cloud computing requirements for consistency with the AF IT Services framework to commercial cloud services.

4.6.6.2.  Coordinate with SAF/AQ and AFMC organizations to ensure a clear, tailorable cost model is established for migration to commercial cloud services.

4.6.7. Implement Network Management (NM) data schemas and net-centric sharing mechanisms to support the development of Service Level Agreements (SLAs), and support the implementation of network management security according to DoDI 8410.03, *Network Management (NM)*.

4.6.8. Ensure that all AF Commercial Cloud Contracts address the additional issues in the DoD Cloud Issue Matrix according to DoD CIO Supplmental Guidance Memo, 16 December 2013.

4.7. **Commander, Air Force Space Command (AFSPC/CC)**. In accordance with AFPD 10-17, AFSPC/CC is responsible for the overall command and control, security and defense of the AFIN.  AFSPC/CC is responsible for the command, control, implementation, security, operation, maintenance, sustainment, configuration, and defense of the AFNET/AFNET-S. These day-to-day authorities may be delegated.  In addition to those responsibilities outlined in 10-series AFIs, AFSPC will:

4.7.1. Assist SAF/CIO A6 to develop policy and guidance for the AFIN and AF adoption of JIE capabilities.

4.7.2. Establish and maintain the Operational Baseline in accordance with AFPD 33-4.

4.7.3. Develop and submit to SAF/CIO A6 and HQ AETC requirements for initial, advanced, supplemental, and qualification training for cyberspace career field members.

4.7.4. Fulfill DoDIN Operations responsibilities for the AFNET/AFNET-S in support of DoDI 8410.02, *NetOps for the Global Information Grid (GIG)*, while remaining consistent with AFPD 10-17, *Cyberspace Operations*, and AFI 10-1701, *Command and Control for Cyberspace Operations*.

4.7.4.1. Establish and provide the necessary resources to ensure compliance with SLAs and memorandums of agreement (MOAs) among DoDIN and JIE service providers and users.

4.7.4.2. Participate in the DoDIN Operations Community of Interest (COI) to share information, promote standards, and resolve DoDIN Operations issues.

4.7.4.3. Participate in the DoD CIO and SAF CIO/A6  Enterprise Architecture (EA) efforts described in DoDI 8410.02 and AFPD 33-4.

4.7.4.4. Ensure all AF contractors and other entities operating AF-owned information systems and AF-controlled information systems on behalf of the Air Force that receive, process, store, display, or transmit AF information, regardless of classification or sensitivity, comply with DoDI 8410.02.

4.7.5. Provide Network Management for the AFNET/AFNET-S with automated Configuration Management and Policy Based Network Management (PBNM) according to DoDI 8410.03.

4.7.6. Ensure the operation of the AF's DoD Internet Services and official use of Internet-based Capabilities (IbC) according to DoDI 8550.01.

4.7.7. Ensure that all DoD Internet services and IbC used by the AF to disseminate unclassified DoD information are assessed at least annually for compliance with DoDI 8550.01.

4.7.8. Provide technical procedures, and standards for the AFIN.

4.7.8.1. Develop MPTOs for AF ITSM to configure, operate, and maintain AF IT established in **Section 5**, AF IT Services Framework.

4.7.8.2. Provide life cycle management of AF ITSM MPTOs with technical content management (TCM) by 24 AF, other subordinate units, AF Program Management Offices (PMOs), or System Program Offices (SPOs) as needed.

4.7.8.3. Serve as the Command Control Point for MPTOs supporting AF ITSM to include technical content management according to TO 00-5-1, *AF Technical Order System*, and TO 00-5-3, *AF Technical Order Lifecycle Management*.

4.7.9. Develop and implement metrics and measures of effectiveness for the AFNET/AFNET-S and AF IT Service Management.

4.7.10. Develop processes and implement policies including MPTOs to manage all AF-owned networks and platform IT interconnections behind appropriate cybersecurity boundaries as defined in the Baselines and according to AFI 33-210, *Air Force Certification and Accreditation Program*.   Review and approve Service Level Agreements for non-AF owned networks on AF installations.

4.7.11. As the AF Authorizing Official (AO) (previously known as Designated Accrediting Authority [DAA]) in accordance with AFI 33-200, assess networthiness and serve as the waiver approval authority for web servers, services, applications, or capabilities supporting the AF to be hosted on commercial servers or services (including cloud computing services) outside of military or government cybersecurity boundaries. The AF AO has responsibility over AF networks, applications and systems as well as the connection approval authority for non-AF systems and applications that will integrate into the AFIN.

4.7.12. Prior to JIE transitions, manage all networks under a One AF-One Network policy by directing the operation, maintenance, and configuration of all AFNET and AFNET-S components (see **Chapter 7**).   Serve as the waiver approval authority for allowing management of networks outside of the lead MAJCOM.

4.7.13. Support and facilitate management of the Standard Desktop Configuration (SDC)/Defense Server Core Configuration (DSCC) by Air Force Enterprise Configuration Management Office (AFECMO).

4.7.14. Ensure records management procedures are implemented and sustained for all enterprise storage services.

4.7.14.1. Ensure technology solutions meet requirements to support eDiscovery capabilities according to DoD 5012.02-STD, *Electronic Records Management Software Applications Design Criteria Standard* and the Federal rules of Civil Proceedure.

4.7.14.2. Implement policy, advocate for resources, and organize, train, and equip cyberspace forces to identify, locate, protect, and produce electronically-stored information in response to litigation requirements.

4.7.14.3. Cooperate with Air Force Legal Operations Agency and the Air Force Records Office directing actions to locate and preserve electronic records as well as non-record electronically stored information which become subject to a litigation hold.

4.7.14.4. Cooperate with Air Force Office of Special Investigations (AFOSI) when an investigation requires the location, acquiring and or preservation of electronic records as well as non-record electronically stored information, IAW AFPD 71-1.

4.7.15. Assist AFMC with the development, integration, testing, and fielding of new systems and services, as required (e.g., step 4 of the SDDP to be published or when requested to determine causes of and solutions to deployment and performance issues).

4.7.16. Incorporate AF IT Services into the Core Functions Support Plan (CFSP), as the CFL for Cyberspace Superiority.

4.7.17. Work with MAJCOM/A6s and Mission/Functional process owners to ensure technical consistency of IT solutions across the AFIN in accordance with AFSPC's roles and responsibilities as CFL for Cyberspace Superiority.

4.7.18. If a specific approval authority is not identified (see **paragraph 4.1.11**), act as the AFIN approval authority for:

   4.7.18.1. System/equipment waiver requests (i.e., purchases, documentation, preventative maintenance inspections).

   4.7.18.2. Proposed temporary modifications, known as T-1 modifications to the AFNET/AFNET-S system/equipment modifications according to AFI 63-131, *Modification Program Management*.

4.7.19. Manage and administer Domain Name Service (DNS) subdomains assigned to the AF by DISA or approved for AF use according to DoDI 8410.01.

   4.7.19.1. Manage AF-level (af.mil and af.smil.mil) DNS and naming convention for the AF according to the MPTO for Directory Services. Maintain a Name Server (NS) record for all AF name servers in the af.mil zone and provide technical support for the af.mil and af.smil.mil domain and sub-domains.

   4.7.19.2. Annually verify administrative and technical contact information is correct in the registrations maintained at the DoD Network Information Center/Secret Internet Protocol Router Network (SIPRNET) Support Center (DoD NIC/SSC) and at the General Services Administration's Government Domain Registration and Services Web site at **http://www.dotgov.gov**.

4.7.20. Review and update AF-level SLAs with external agencies and supported MAJCOMs as required.

4.7.21. Provide network integration and engineering services for the AFNET/AFNET-S and development of JIE capabilities.

   4.7.21.1. Ensure operational systems do not introduce vulnerabilities to the AFNET/AFNET-S or disrupt existing functions, while creating a resilient network environment that preserves operational advantage.

   4.7.21.2. Perform networthiness consultation, validation, compliance and assessments of risk to the AFIN to enforce standards for functional and cyberspace systems, applications, and products requiring connection to the AFIN.

   4.7.21.3. Develop and implement the AFNET Integration Process to verify compliance with security, interoperability, supportability, sustainability, usability regulations of systems, applications, and/or products, and readiness review criteria.

   4.7.21.4. Collaborate with organizations to integrate all AF-owned, contracted or developed systems into the AFNET/AFNET-S.

   4.7.21.5. Develop integration and implementation plans for AFIN & AFNET evolution to current and future JIE capabilities.

4.7.22. Provide the AF's engineering center of excellence for developing and implementing technical solutions for the AFIN via subordinate organizations such as the 38th Cyberspace Engineering Installation Group (38 CEIG) and AF Network Integration Center (AFNIC).

4.7.22.1. Document Main Operating Base AFIN infrastructure, including system life-cycle information, via the Cyberspace Infrastructure Planning System (CIPS) (Reference MPTO 00-33D-3003, *Managing the Cyberspace Infrastructure with the Cyberspace Infrastructure Planning System*).

4.7.22.2. Provide AFIN network operations with enterprise engineering services according to AFI 33-150, *Management of Cyberspace Support Activities*.

4.7.22.3. Develop and analyze cyberspace requirements and associated impacts on operational architectures and capabilities, and convert AF and DoD technical specifications into standard AFIN and joint solutions to facilitate convergence on a single robust and defensible architecture.

4.7.22.4. Provide network health and vulnerability assessments as coordinated and directed by 24 AF/AFCYBER, including network security and optimization assistance as well as event-driven response action teams.

4.7.22.5. Develop and maintain the AFNET Infrastructure Roadmap and AFNET Concept of Operations to serve as an input to the Target Baseline and show how the Operational Baseline would evolve into the Target Baseline. The Roadmap and Concept of Operations will address Cyber, Situational Awareness of the network, and Network Management capabilities as well as operational roles and responsibilities. The Infrastructure Roadmap will contain the collected and prioritized set of requirements.

4.8. **24th Air Force (24 AF (AFCYBER)).** 24 AF is the AF component to USCYBERCOM. AFSPC/CC may delegate certain authorities to 24 AF/CC IAW AFI 10-1701, Command and Control for Cyberspace Operations.

4.8.1. In coordination with AFSPC, maintain and administer the Operational Baseline including the AFNET/AFNET-S.

4.8.2. Serve as liaison between the AFECMO and the operational community to facilitate the development and implementation of the SDC/DSCC.

4.8.3. Direct the security, operations, and defense of cloud computing services operated for the AF outside of AF network boundaries but logically a part of the AFIN, using authorities designated by the Cyber C2 structure in AFI 10-1701.

4.8.4. Provide assessments of impact to the AFIN in response to requests for web servers, services, applications, or capabilities to be hosted on commercial servers or services outside of military or government cybersecurity boundaries.

4.8.5. In coordination with AFSPC, review and approve/disapprove MAJCOM unique applications, communications systems, and IT Services requests/needs to ensure compatibility with AF IT Services. Include recommended changes affected by use of commercial servers or services (including cloud computing services).

4.8.6. Provide enterprise-level management of AF IT Services.

4.8.7. Monitor subordinate units' compliance with orders issued and provide assistance on compliance issues when resolution is beyond their scope and/or resources.

4.9. **624th Operations Center (624 OC).** 624 OC is the operational-level C2 organization for 24 AF (AFCYBER), providing strategy, planning, execution monitoring and assessment of Air Force cyber operations. 624 OC directs AF cyber operations and the activities of subordinate 24 AF cyber units via the Cyber Tasking Order (CTO) and other cyber orders. In addition to duties specified in 10-series AFIs and applicable CYBERCOM orders, 624 OC is responsible for the following:

4.9.1. Develop options and directs operational configuration changes, Information Operations Condition (INFOCON) changes (see AFI 10-710, *Information Operations Condition (INFOCON)*), and changes to security postures in response to vulnerabilities and incidents, AF and CCMD operations, USCYBERCOM direction, and outages that cross MAJCOMs, affect the preponderance of the AFIN, or are time critical in nature.

4.9.2. Perform trend analysis and correlation of threat, performance, and compliance metrics as it relates to Vulnerability Management.

4.10. **Major Commands (MAJCOMs)/Functionals.** MAJCOMs/Functionals implement AF guidance concerning the operation and maintenance of mission specific MAJCOM/Functional unique applications, communications systems, and IT. MAJCOMs/Functionals will:

4.10.1. Manage and provide support for command/functional-unique programs and systems/IT. **(T-1).**

4.10.1.1. Ensure command/functional-unique programs and systems/IT integrate with, but do not conflict with applicable AF IT Services. **(T-1).**

4.10.1.2. Ensure command/functional-unique applications do not duplicate infrastructure, services or capabilities provided by the AFIN, AFNET, AFNET-S or JIE, by reviewing the Target, Implementation, and Operational Baselines for planned or existing services or capabilities. Exceptions must be approved by SAF/CIO A6. **(T-1).**

4.10.1.3. Conduct application rationalization within their portfolios for business and mission systems to eliminate duplicity and ensure proper alignment with their business process in accordance with AFI 33-141, *Air Force Information Technology Portfolio Management and IT Investment Review.* **(T-1).**

4.10.1.4. Ensure new applications and systems are fielded within IPNs, CDCs or the MilCloud, SPPNs, Tactical Processing Nodes TPNs, or the Commercial Cloud IAW AF and DoD guidance. **(T-0).**

4.10.2. Utilize only AFECMO produced standard configurations for command-unique systems. Cloning, repackaging, adding, or removing software from AFECMO standard images with the intent of producing a customized image is strictly prohibited except as waived by the AF AO (previously known as DAA) according to paragraph 4.15.2. **(T-1).**

4.10.3. Submit requests to change an Operational Baseline Configuration Item (CI) such as new software or an equipment upgrade. **(T-1)**.

4.10.3.1. For non-program office fielded systems, follow the Change Management process by using the change request module of the Enterprise Information Technology Service Manager (EITSM), a.k.a. Remedy, or via AFTO Form 265, *Request for Change,* according to MPTO 00-33A-1100, *Change Management,*.

4.10.3.2. For program office fielded systems and equipment, submit AF Form 1067 according to AFI 63-131, *Modification Program Management*.

4.10.4. Plan, program, and budget for the capability to respond to orders released according to AFI 10-1701, that impact command/functional-unique programs and systems/equipment including end user workstations and/or network servers and localized infrastructure supporting command-unique requirements. **(T-1)**.

4.10.5. Designate a MAJCOM/AF Forces Communications Control Center (M/ACCC) or equivalent organization to function as the MAJCOM's advocate for mission impacts to the user community (MAJCOM only). **(T-1)**.

4.11. **MAJCOM/AF Forces Communications Control Centers (M/ACCCs) will:**

4.11.1. As an operational element of the MAJCOM Commander's staff , combine situational awareness of networks and information systems supporting the MAJCOM with an in-depth MAJCOM-unique understanding of how those networks and systems are used to accomplish the mission of the command. **(T-2)**.

4.11.2. Generate and disseminate near-real time situational awareness of how MAJCOM missions are being delayed, disrupted, degraded, or terminated due to events associated with the underlying communications networks critical to those missions. **(T-2)**.

4.11.3. Serve as the information dissemination point of contact to the Integrated Network Operations and Security Centers (I-NOSCs), Enterprise Service Units (ESUs), and AF Enterprise Service Desk (ESD) on mission impacts and/or degradation to the mission and its user community. **(T-1)**.

4.11.4. Elevate issues beyond the bases' responsibility or capability to the respective enterprise service support organization. **(T-2)**.

4.12. **Communications Focal Point (CFP) within the Communications Squadron or equivalent will:**

4.12.1. Serve as the conduit for the AF ESD to resolve communications systems and equipment issues at base level. The AF ESD is responsible for all AFNET users, but will delegate some of that responsibility to the CFPs via the Federated Administrative Rights (FAR). Tools such as Information Assurance Officer Express (IAO Express) and Virtual ESD (vESD) will automate certain functions, then re-route tickets that cannot be handled by the tool to either the CFP for Tier 1 or Tier 2 support, as appropriate and/or depending on the FAR authorized, or to the ESD backshop for further processing/support. Tickets that are routed to the CFP will then be routed (by the CFP) to the appropriate production work center for resolution. **(T-1)**.

4.12.2. Operate systems and the AFNET/AFNET-S in the IPN according to AFIN baseline management processes and AF IT Services MPTOs. **(T-1)**.

4.12.3. Maintain accountability of all AFIN components physically present on the installation regardless of the organization operating the equipment. (T-1).

4.12.4. Execute control of production procedures prescribed by AFI 33-150 and MPTO 00-33A-1001, *General Cyberspace Support Activities Management Procedures and Practice Requirements.* Execute control of production on AFNET/AFNET-S components when requested by the operating organization, such as the 26 NOS, I-NOSCs or 33 NWS. Control of production includes planning and scheduling production, ordering and managing materials, and maintaining Automated Information Systems (AISs). **(T-2)**.

4.12.5. Serve as or assign a performing workcenter to provide preventive and touch maintenance on AFNET/AFNET-S, functional, and PMO equipment only as directed by the owning organization (e.g., I-NOSC, ESU, 26 NOS, 33 NWS, MAJCOM, PMO). **(T-1)**.

4.12.6. Utilize only AFECMO produced standard configurations (e.g., SDC, DSCC). Cloning, repackaging, adding, or removing software from AFECMO standard images with the intent of producing a customized image is strictly prohibited except as waived by the AF AO (previously known as DAA) according to **paragraph 4.15.2**. **(T-1)**.

4.12.7. Provide detailed maintenance records in a transferable system such as Remedy for preventive and touch maintenance on AFNET/AFNET-S equipment when directed to execute such maintenance by the owning organization. Utilize Integrated Maintenance Data System (IMDS) for all maintenance data tracking and actions completed on the AISs within physical control of CFP, according to MPTO 00-33A-1001. **(T-2)**.

4.12.8. Elevate issues beyond the base's responsibility or capability to the respective enterprise service support organization. **(T-1)**.

4.12.9. Execute actions to comply with Cyber C2 orders according to **paragraph 7**. **(T-1)**.

4.12.9.1. Identify information systems controlled by a PMO which will only be patched or modified upon approval of the PMO or system owner. **(T-1)**.

4.12.9.2. For command/functional systems, coordinate with Functional System Administrators (FSAs) to take action to comply with Cyber C2 orders. **(T-1)**.

4.12.10. Where remote administration/connectivity fails to resolve an end user service incident or fulfill a AF ITSM responsibility (e.g., Vulnerability Management), the CFP can be assigned network permissions and responsibilities to troubleshoot and resolve end user service incidents or fulfill AF ITSM responsibilities. Perform actions within local control requiring a touch labor solution as directed. **(T-1)**.

4.12.10.1. Document tasking and effort using Service Incident Management and Problem Management where appropriate.

4.12.11. Identify and resolve network threats, vulnerabilities, and attacks in coordination with the I-NOSCs, so as to minimize risks to operations. **(T-1)**.

4.12.12. Inform base leadership and base populace on network threats, vulnerabilities, and actions. **(T-2)**.

4.12.13. Notify/coordinate Authorized Service Interruptions (ASI) to minimize impact on base-level mission. **(T-1)**.

4.12.14. Maintain situational awareness of their portion of the AFIN. Notify I-NOSCs and M/ACCCs of any issues regarding equipment under CFP control or that may affect base users. **(T-1)**.

4.12.15. Report communications systems/equipment issues to MAJCOM and other higher headquarter functions as required. The CFP will provide situational awareness to the M/ACCC according to MAJCOM or Combatant Commanders guidance. **(T-1)**.

4.12.16. Coordinate, correlate, assess de-conflict and eradicate suspicious/malicious activity through appropriate authorities FSAs, M/ACCC, 561 NOS, 83 NOS, 299 NOSS and 33 NWS. **(T-2)**.

4.12.17. Perform information dissemination management. **(T-2)**.

4.12.18. Follow compliance reporting requirements as specified in each Cyber C2 order. Orders may require compliance-based, task-based, or asset-based reporting. **(T-1)**.

4.12.19. Develop and exercise COOPs. **(T-3)**. The Communications Squadron/equivalent Plans office will take lead on the development and maintenance of COOPs and/or Disaster Recovery Plan (DRP) for managed services. Work centers will assist the Plans office with the COOP/DRP development for services under their responsibility. COOP will focus on restoring an organization's mission-essential functions (MEF) at an alternate site and performing those functions for up to 30 days before returning to normal operations. See National Institute of Standards and Technology (NIST) Special Publication 800-34, Contingency Planning Guide for Information Technology Systems, for more details.

4.12.20. Up channel information that may help C2 of the AFIN. **(T-2)**.

4.13. AF Enterprise Configuration Management Office (AFECMO).

4.13.1. AFECMO will provide configuration management of the Standard Desktop Configuration (SDC), Defense Server Core Configuration (DSCC), Systems Center Configuration Manager (SCCM) and associated Group Policies, software components and TOs. **(T-1)**.

4.13.2. AFECMO is the only organization authorized to make changes to the SDC and DSCC installation image/configuration, baseline group policy, or the SCCM configuration baseline  except as approved by the AFSPC Operational Baseline process or directed through orders released according to AFI 10-1701. Any organization cloning, repackaging, adding, or removing software from AFECMO standard images with the intent of producing a customized image is strictly prohibited except as waived by the AF AO (previously known as DAA). **(T-1)**.

4.14. **Air Force Program Management Offices (PMOs), System Program Offices (SPOs), and Organizations Developing, and/or Managing, Operating non-core IT Services, Applications or Capabilities.** Note: In accordance with the acquisition chain of authority and acquisition requirements specified in AFI 63-101/20-101, tiering of the acquisition requirements does not apply and waiver authority resides with the program execution chain. This does not relieve the program execution chain of complying with IT Services requirements specified in AFI 33-115. These organizations will:

4.14.1. Design, build, and sustain AFIN components and systems in accordance with the Implementation Baseline. Ensure infrastructure, services or capabilities are not duplicated from those provided by the AFIN or the JIE, by reviewing the Target, Implementation, and Operational Baselines for planned or existing services or capabilities. Exceptions must be approved by SAF/CIO A6. **(T-1)**.

4.14.2. Design, build, and sustain systems and associated IT according to IT baseline management processes, AF IT Services MPTOs, systems TOs, and guidance for Integrated Life Cycle Management (ILCM) provided by AFPD 63-1/20-1, *Integrated Life Cycle Management*. **(T-1)**.

4.14.2.1. Ensure information systems environments are developed and maintained consistent with the AFIN technical architecture published as the Target, Implementation, and Operational Baselines according to AFPD 33-4, where applicable, for AF capabilities built on cloud services.

4.14.2.2. Evaluate cloud computing solutions in accordance with **paragraph 5.3**, as part of their planning process when developing new applications or evaluating changes to the hosting of existing applications. Rationalize existing application needs, virtualize, and migrate existing applications to approved data centers and/or cloud services to support AF data center consolidation goals. The requiring program office is responsible for the acquisition and funding of cloud computing as supporting infrastructure. **(T-0)**.

4.14.3. Comply with all Cyber C2 orders according to **paragraph 7**. **(T-1)**.

4.14.4. Implement all actions required by Cyber C2 orders directing AF ITSM (e.g., Vulnerability Management) and report compliance/non-compliance according to the orders and applicable methods and procedures. **(T-1)**.

4.14.5. Host, tenant, and Geographically Separated Unit (GSU) organizations will coordinate all IT actions with potential impact on the network or other IT services or capabilities with their servicing CFP. **(T-1)**.

4.14.6. Utilize AFECMO produced standard configurations (e.g., SDC, DSCC). Cloning, repackaging, adding, or removing software from AFECMO standard images with the intent of producing a customized image is strictly prohibited except as waived by the AF AO (previously known as DAA) according to **paragraph 4.13.2**. **(T-1)**.

4.14.7. Conform to a One AF-One Network policy (see **paragraph 7.6**) managed by AFSPC. All systems on the network must be configured to operate within this construct or possess a waiver from the lead MAJCOM. **(T-1)**.

4.14.8. Utilize base CFP, ESU, I-NOSC, DISA, or other government enterprise managed network services and Enterprise Core Services. IT capabilities or data servers residing outside the protections of government networks and data centers require a waiver from the lead MAJCOM. **(T-1)**.

4.14.8.1. Manage all data servers and associated computing infrastructure in the data center (IPN, SPPN) as approved by the ITGEB in support of federal and AF efforts to reduce operating costs by consolidating data centers. **(T-0)**.

4.14.8.2. Submit requirements for required approvals of data servers and associated IT using CIPS through the base level Cyberspace Systems Integrator (CSI) according to AFI 33-150, **Attachment 2**. Obligation requests must be submitted to **usaf.pentagon.saf-cio-a6.mbx.a3c-a6c-afdcc-workflow@mail.mil** and approved by the servicing lead command or MAJCOM A6. **(T-1)**.

4.14.9. Provide Information Support Plans to AFIN Operations activities as required by AFI 63-101/20-101, *Integrated Life Cycle Management,* for any IT system that exchanges information external to itself, and/or is connected to the DoDIN.

**4.15. Functional Systems Administrator (FSA) will:**

4.15.1. Ensure functional communities of interest systems, servers, workstations, peripherals, communications devices, and software are on-line and supported. **(T-2)**.

4.15.2. Manage and maintain their functional systems. Provide an interface between program representatives and the CFP, CDC, or IPN. **(T-1)**.

4.15.3. Create a SLA or MOA for any transfer of administrative responsibilities to an IPN. **(T-2)**.

4.15.3.1. Implement all actions required by Cyber C2 orders as approved by each system's configuration control authority according to **paragraph 7**. **(T-1)**. Coordinate order implementation with servicing CFP, I-NOSC, users, and external agencies.

4.15.3.2. Follow compliance reporting requirements as specified in each Cyber C2 order. Orders may require compliance-based, task-based, or asset-based reporting.

4.15.4. Work with the CFP to:

4.15.4.1. Eradicate malicious logic from networks, information systems, and stand-alone computing devices. **(T-1)**.

4.15.4.2. Assess the scope of unauthorized network activities or incidents. **(T-1)**.

4.15.4.3. Review and upchannel I-NOSC-run vulnerability reports to the owning PMO.

4.15.5. Utilize AFECMO produced standard configurations (e.g., SDC, DSCC). Cloning, repackaging, adding, or removing software from AFECMO standard images with the intent of producing a customized image is strictly prohibited except as waived by the AF AO (previously known as DAA) according to **paragraph 4.13.2**. **(T-1)**.

**4.16. All Unit Commanders will:**

4.16.1. Ensure assigned personnel use government provided equipment, government IT services, or Internet-based Capabilities accessed from government equipment for official, authorized, or limited authorized personal use according to AFMAN 33-152 and DoDI 8550.01. **(T-0)**.

4.16.2. Maintain the security, integrity, and accountability of AF information on the Internet by establishing and maintaining public websites/capabilities inside the network demilitarized zone (DMZ) and private websites/capabilities inside the protections of government network security. Any AF website, servers, services, applications, or capabilities to be hosted on commercial servers or services outside of military or government cybersecurity boundaries requires AFSPC lead command approval. **(T-0)**.

4.16.3. Ensure all publically accessible DoD Internet Services managed by the organization comply with applicable cybersecurity controls, information security procedures, OPSEC measures, and DoDI 8550.01 requirements including registration and dissemination guidance. **(T-0)**.

4.16.4. Control content on public websites through the Public Affairs (PA) office according to AFI 35-107, *Public Web Communications* and AFI 35-102, *Security and Policy Review Process*. **(T-0)**.

4.16.5. Ensure all public websites and capabilities within the organization span of control are submitted to wing/base PA offices for review prior to their launch. ANG units will coordinate with their unit Public Affairs Officer (PAO) prior to their launch. ANG geographically separated units use their host wing for PAO support. **(T-0)**.

4.16.6. Obtain all Internet connectivity and web services through the supporting base CFP except as excluded by paragraph 7.4 **(T-2)**.

**4.17. Air Force Office of Special Investigations Cyber Investigations and Operations (AFOSI CI&O).** AFOSI conducts cyber investigations and operations in, through, and beyond cyberspace to identify, exploit, and neutralize criminal, terrorist, and intelligence threats to the AF, DoD, and US Government (USG). Air Force Mission Directive (AFMD) 39, *Air Force Office of Special Investigations (AFOSI),* and Air Force Policy Directive (AFPD) 71-1, *Criminal Investigations and Counterintelligence*, both implement DoDD O-5240.02, *Counterintelligence*, and define AFOSI's role as the Air Force's sole agency for conducting counterintelligence (CI) investigations, and offensive counterintelligence operations (OFCO) and as such is the only Air Force agency authorized to do so in cyberspace. AFOSI is also responsible for initiating and conducting independent criminal investigations per AFMD 39 and AFPD 71-1. The CI&O program is AFOSI's primary cybercrime investigative and operations capability. For the purposes of this paragraph, AFOSI is a DoD intelligence component as defined in DoD 5240.1-R, *Procedures Governing the Activities of DoD Intelligence Components That Affect United States Persons*. AFOSI CI&O will:

4.17.1. Be the focal point for Law Enforcement (LE) and Counterintelligence activities in cyberspace and the AFIN.

4.17.2. Provide Law Enforcement support to AFCYBER/CC for matters occurring in or impacting the AFIN.

4.17.3. Provide Cyber Counterintelligence support to AFCYBER/CC and the AF for matters occurring in or impacting the AFIN.

**5. AF IT Services Framework.** The AF IT Services Framework, as an ITSM framework, provides foundation which integrates and manages the AFIN, enterprise core services, and solutions to support the AF portion of the DoDIN and the DoD Information Enterprise as defined by DoDD 8000.01.   AF IT Services are functionally aligned to the Defense Information Enterprise Architecture and its activities.   AF IT Services may not be provided by a single entity but are instead a federated, shared capability among several organizations.  The services will be developed, operated and maintained in accordance with the Target, Implementation, and Operational Baselines and the processes defined by this publication and supporting MPTOs. Mission/Functional Unique Applications may be supported and defined as a new AF IT Services as their usage and scope increases across the enterprise supporting the AF usage of a previously functional unique application.  Additional AF IT Services will be initially designated in the Target or Implementation Baseline as appropriate with requests and changes to the Baselines managed by the Air Force Consolidated Enterprise Information Technology Baseline (AF CEITB).

**Figure 2.  AF IT Services Framework.**

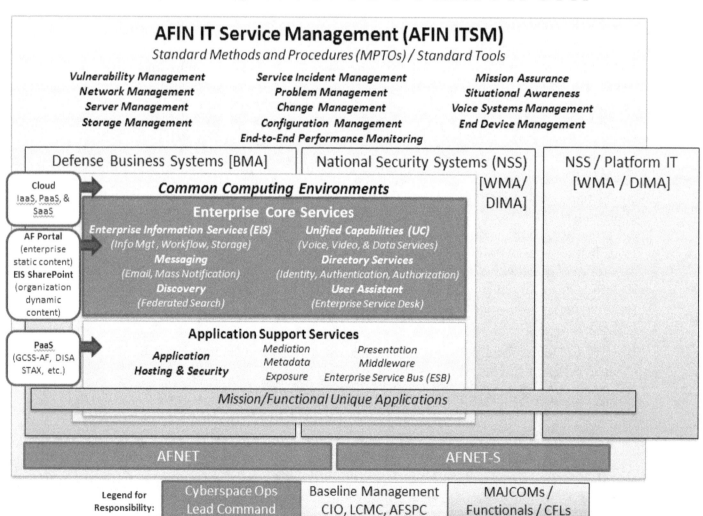

5.1. **AF IT Services Management (AF ITSM).** AF IT Service Management is established as IT components, infrastructure, and processes (e.g., Network Management, Vulnerability Management) enabling effective operations and defense of the AFIN and the IT services. AF IT Service Management creates a trusted environment capable of protecting and maintaining the integrity, quality, and availability of the AFIN. All terrestrial, space and airborne networks will inherit the capabilities of AF IT Service Management, reference AFPD 33-5, *Warfighting Integration* for establishment of a fully integrated, flexible and net-centric family of systems, networks and architectures bridging theater warfighting, combat support, global/functional capabilities and infrastructure enterprises. Non-traditional services that are being migrated onto the Internet Protocol (IP) network (e.g., IP telephony, video teleconferencing) will need to be managed for both non-standard or legacy systems and newer IP-based implementations until all legacy systems are removed from the AF.

5.1.1. **Vulnerability Management**. Vulnerability Management is established as the practice of identifying AFIN hardware and software vulnerabilities, performing risk analysis, prioritizing mitigation actions based on levels of risk deemed acceptable by an appropriate commander, and remediating and/or mitigating the vulnerabilities to proactively prevent exploitation. This service area includes all AFIN systems and components, and the complete cycle of identification, classification, remediation, and mitigation of vulnerabilities. Vulnerability Management also includes patching, tracking, and testing. *Note: Special precautions are taken with Command, Control, Intelligence, Surveillance, and Reconnaissance mission systems and non-standard or legacy systems to ensure automated vulnerability fix actions do not degrade operational missions.* Specific methods and procedures are in MPTO 00-33A-1109, *Vulnerability Management*.

5.1.2. **Network Management**. Network Management is established as the ability to monitor, control, configure, and optimize networks, systems, services and the underlying physical assets that provide end-user services, as well as connectivity to enterprise application services all in accordance with the applicable DISA Security Technical Implementation Guides (STIGs). Network Management includes the activities, methods, processes, procedures, capabilities, tools, and resources that pertain to the operation, administration, logging, maintenance, and provisioning of networked systems. Network Management begins with the background situational awareness of network configuration and performance of networks. Network Management shall have and use automated Configuration Management and PBNM according to DoDI 8410.03. Specific procedures are in MPTO 00-33A-1106, *Air Force Information Network (AFIN) Network Management*.

5.1.3. **Server Management**. Server Management is established as the activities, methods, processes, procedures, capabilities, tools, and resources that pertain to the operation, administration, monitoring, configuration, and maintenance of the hardware and software components of a server in accordance with the applicable DISA STIGs. Server Management includes coordination of server requirements for environmental and facility support, installation and deployment, monitoring, configuration, and security. Specific methods and procedures for Server Management are in MPTO 00-33A-1113, *AFIN Server/Storage Management and Application Hosting*.

5.1.4. **Storage Management**. Storage Management is established as the activities, methods, processes, procedures, capabilities, tools, and resources that provide for the storage, retrieval, availability, backup and recovery, destruction, labeling, quota management, security, and confidentiality of user data on the AFIN in accordance with the applicable STIGs. Storage Management also includes the administration, configuration, and monitoring of the storage media and devices. Specific methods and procedures for Storage Management are in MPTO 00-33A-1113, *AFIN Server/Storage Management and Application Hosting.*

5.1.5. **Service Incident Management**. Service Incident Management is established as the activities, methods, processes, procedures, capabilities, tools, and resources used to restore normal service operations as quickly as possible. A service incident is any event (network security, network management, etc.) which is not part of standard operations and causes an interruption or reduction of the quality of service. A service incident is categorized under three major ticket models as Standard (applications, services, networks, etc.), Major (accelerated workflow with reduced escalation timelines), or Security (handling follows security incident guidance) with separate procedures and workflows for each major type. The goal of Service Incident Management is to minimize the adverse effect on operations, ensuring the best possible levels of service and availability are maintained. Service Incident Management is directly linked to management of the physical infrastructure and should focus on identifying infrastructure issues and documenting corrective actions or changes needed to prevent incidents in the future. Specific procedures for Service Incident Management are in the MPTO 00-33A-1112, *Air Force Network Enterprise Service Desk Service Incident Management.* Security incident procedures will be published in MPTO 00-33B-5007, *Security Incident Management for Information Systems.* Cyber incident procedures will be published in AFI 10-1702, *Cyber Incident Handling.*

5.1.6. **Problem Management**. Problem Management is established as the activities, methods, processes, procedures, capabilities, tools, and resources used to identify and resolve the root causes of service incidents and prevent their recurrence. A "problem" is a condition typically identified as a result of multiple service incidents that exhibit common symptoms, share related mission impacts, or share a common root cause. Problem Management includes event correlation, trend analysis, problem diagnosis, root cause analysis, and knowledge basing to provide a user-level knowledge base of answers and resolutions to common user-level issues. Specific procedures for Problem Management are in MPTO 00-33A-1114, *AFIN Problem Management.*

5.1.7. **Change Management**. Change Management is established as standardized activities, methods, processes, and procedures used to effectively manage and control all changes to the AFIN Operational Baseline, minimizing risk, disruptions in service and adverse impacts to operational users. A "change" is the addition, modification or removal of anything that could have an effect on IT services, configuration, processes, security, etc. Change Management focuses on documenting changes to the network. This includes documenting updates made to maps, drawings, network layouts, Virtual Local Area Network (VLAN) Architectures, IP addresses, and network configurations. Linkages identified such as base level drawings must be included in the CSI blueprint. The change management process must begin at the base level and extend to the AF level to ensure all requirements are contained in one process. Multiple change management processes must be consolidated and a governing group be formed to focus on change management. Change management and configuration management must be a dynamic process. Any change to the network must be automatically reflected in the visualization of the network configuration. It is critical to clarify the relationship between change management and vulnerability management. Vulnerability management is change management responsiveness to security-directed changes. Specific procedures for Change Management are published in MPTO 00-33A-1100, *AF-GIG Operational Change Management Process*.

5.1.8. **Configuration Management**. Configuration Management is established as the activities, methods, processes, procedures, capabilities, tools, and resources which establish and maintain thorough, documented baselines of the hardware and software configuration items of the AFIN, including the features, attributes, technical configuration, and documentation of the components. Configuration Management defines those items that are configurable, those items that require formal change control, and the process for controlling changes to such items. Configuration Management is vital to network and system stability and will be automated to support Network Management according to DoDI 8410.03. Before changes are introduced into a network or system, they must be properly reviewed, approved and documented following Change Management methods and procedures. Specific procedures for Configuration Management will be in the *Configuration Management MPTO*.

5.1.9. **End-to-End Performance Monitoring**. End-to-End Performance Monitoring is established as deliberate, proactive monitoring and capacity planning of all the hardware and software components of the AFIN which enables all AF IT Services including mission/functional unique applications. It supports mission assurance by including the end user experience and the warfighter's ability to access critical information. End-to-End Performance Monitoring includes the activities, methods, processes, procedures, capabilities, tools, and resources which allow cyber professionals to rapidly identify, isolate, and resolve service incidents before they cause significant degradation or poor performance resulting in mission impact. Monitoring, measuring, performance analysis, and optimizing networks and networked systems are included in the scope. Capacity Planning includes the long trend analysis of network devices including servers, and should be performed in order to identify future constraints with the results incorporated into either future Technical Baselines. Service and application performance is affected by both the performance of the network and performance of the servers and applications providing the service. As the operator of the network, 24 AF has the ultimate responsibility for determining the network elements to be monitored, the thresholds that must be established, and the appropriate responses to results that fall outside the established thresholds. 24 AF must coordinate with the network owner (e.g., DISA, Army, etc.) if monitoring spans networks outside of AF control. End-to-End Performance Monitoring applies to the NIPRNET and the SIPRNET, and all other terrestrial, space and airborne networks – anywhere a network can be hosted – for all entities (Active, Guard, & Reserve). Specific procedures for End-to-End Performance Monitoring will be in the *End-to-End Performance Monitoring MPTO*.

5.1.10. **Mission Assurance**. Mission Assurance is established as the actions taken to ensure operational users can leverage AFIN systems and command/functional unique systems to execute operational missions. This includes activities, methods, processes, procedures, capabilities, tools, and resources that protect and defend information and information systems by ensuring their availability, integrity, authentication, confidentiality, and non-repudiation. Continuity of operations, disaster recovery, risk management, and "fighting through an attack" are also critical aspects of Mission Assurance. Mission Assurance requires traceability of mission dependencies on cyberspace capabilities to provide prioritization of all other AFIN activities and provide the mission context for Situational Awareness. This applies to all components of the AF IT Services Framework. Specific procedures for Mission Assurance will be in the *Mission Assurance and Situational Awareness MPTO.*

5.1.11. **Situational Awareness**. Cyberspace Situational Awareness (SA) is the requisite current and predictive knowledge of cyberspace and the operating environment upon which cyberspace operations depend, including all factors affecting friendly and adversary cyberspace forces (JP 3-12). Situational Awareness is enabled by the activities, methods, processes, procedures, capabilities, tools, and resources which provide meaningful and relevant end-to-end visibility incorporating data from End-to-End Performance Monitoring and other management data into a common operational picture by providing the operating status, location, performance, and utilization of AFIN hardware and software, both (a) within context as AFIN resources and (b) within the context of the mission(s) those resources are supporting. Specific procedures for Situational Awareness will be in the *Mission Assurance & Situational Awareness MPTO.*

5.1.12. **Voice Systems Management.** Voice Systems Management is established as the ability to monitor, control, configure, and optimize voice systems. Voice Systems Management includes the activities, methods, processes, procedures, capabilities, tools, and resources that pertain to the operation, administration, maintenance, and provisioning of voice systems. Voice Systems Management will be undergoing significant change as a part of the DoD category of Unified Capabilities (UC), as stated in the AF UC Master Plan and DoDI 8100.04, *DoD Unified Capabilities (UC).* To optimize support of real-time voice (video, etc.) requirements in the future, systems and data networks must be optimized to meet the unique requirements of UC while eliminating specific system stovepipes to provide quality of service (QoS) needs for Voice over Internet Protocol (VoIP) and UC. Additional guidance for Voice Systems Management is available in AFMAN 33-145, *Collaboration Services and Voice Systems Management.* Specific procedures for Voice Systems Management will be in MPTO 00-33A-1108 *Voice Systems Management.*

5.1.13. **End Device Management**. End Device Management is established as the installation and deployment, monitoring, configuration, maintenance, and security of end devices on the AFIN. End devices are items such as desktop PCs, laptops, notebooks, tablet PCs, smartphones, executive mobile devices, VoIP phones, IP-enabled sensors/alarms, etc. Specific procedures for End Device Management will be in the *End Device Management MPTO.*

5.2. **Enterprise Core Services**. Enterprise Core Services are standard IT capabilities available to all users on the AFIN. Enterprise Core Services support DoD Net-Centric strategies for data and services by enabling users to safeguard, compile, catalog, discover, cache, distribute, retrieve, and share data in a collaborative environment across the AF and DoD enterprises. As DoD establishes joint enterprise services under JIE, the AF will evaluate the transition of AF enterprise core services when appropriate. 24AF will operate AF enterprise services not provided by JIE, and/or those JIE enterprise services being provided by the AF to all DoD customers.

5.2.1. **Collaboration**. Collaboration services are established as the capabilities and resources that allow communications and interactions across the AFIN enterprise, including voice, video, data, and visual representation. This includes those capabilities which may be bundled into Unified Capabilities (UC). UC are defined as the integration of voice, video, and/or data services delivered ubiquitously across a secure and highly available network infrastructure, independent of technology, to provide increased mission effectiveness to the warfighter and business communities (DOD Unified Capabilities Requirements 2013). Examples may include web conferencing, application and desktop sharing, presence, chat, video teleconferencing, VoIP, white boarding, chat rooms, and online forums. Additional guidance for Collaboration is in AFMAN 33-145, *Collaboration Services and Voice Systems Management* and DoDI 8100.04, *DoD Unified Capabilities (UC)*.

5.2.2. **Messaging**. Messaging services are established as the exchange of electronic message traffic between all users and organizational entities on the AFIN. Messaging services include the ability to compose, read, store, forward, manage, prioritize, digitally sign/encrypt, and track delivery/receipt of electronic messages. The AF is transitioning messaging services to cloud services utilitzing DISA Enterprise Email (DEE). Examples may include email, Instant Messaging and Voicemail. Specific user procedures for Messaging are in AFMAN 33-152, *User Responsibilities and Guidance for Information Systems* and incorporated in UC covered by AFMAN 33-145.

5.2.3. **Discovery**. Discovery services are established as the capabilities and resources that enable users to identify, search, locate, and retrieve information across the AFIN. Discovery services include the ability to catalog and index information, identify applicable data repositories, formulate search queries/criteria, and retrieve/deliver relevant information to users in a timely fashion. This is a critical capability enabler for change management, configuration management, policy based management, and performance analysis as described above. Specific procedures for Discovery will be in the *Discovery and Information Management MPTO*.

5.2.4. **Enterprise Information Services (EIS)**. Enterprise Information Services will provide a solution across the entire AF by enabling organizations to communicate and collaborate vertically and horizontally with all EIS capabilities, optimizing the use of available bandwidth by using the most effective capabilities for the operational environment. Warfighters will utilize Knowledge Operations (KO) capabilities to drive operational effects through improved decision-making processes. Warfighters will pull required information and knowledge smartly, push information for continuous collaboration across the unified communications domain, and receive the right information at the right time and in the right format through advanced collaboration techniques (i.e., integrated people, processes and technology) via a proactive push from all integrated operations and support functions. Enterprise Information Services effectively capitalize upon KO performed by commanders, who integrate all AF functional areas into refined staff organizations, internal battle rhythms, and routine interactive sessions with subordinate commanders worldwide. The KO vision of a "One AF—One Enterprise" to fundamentally change the way the AF uses, delivers, and manages knowledge to perform peacetime missions and wartime operations across an integrated AF enterprise recognizes the imperative for a proactive means to promote collaboration, the sharing of ideas, and to find solutions to common problems across the entire AF. It also promotes the ability to learn, innovate, decide, and act, faster than our adversaries while operating in a condition of persistent conflict. Enterprise Information Services are established as the capabilities and resources supporting the security, reliable storage, timely delivery and deduplication of information across the AFIN enterprise. Examples include common and private data/file service, workflow management service, and enterprise print service. These services will be implemented and sustained according to AFPD 33-3, *Information Management*. Specific procedures for Information Management will be in the *Discovery and Information Management MPTO*.

**5.2.5. Knowledge Management (KM).** Knowledge Management (KM) is the capturing, organizing, and storing of knowledge and experiences of individual workers and groups within an organization and making this information available to others in the organization. KM is the art of creating, organizing, applying, and transferring knowledge to facilitate situational understanding and decision making. (AFSPC Enabling Concept for Knowledge Operations, May 2011)

**5.2.6. Application Hosting.** Application Hosting services are established as hosting environments that are architecturally compliant, consistent, reliable, and secure computing environments (consisting of application software and associated utilities) supporting AF IT Services, Enterprise Core Services, Application Support Services, and mission/functional unique applications and systems. All Application Hosting will migrate to Common Computing Environments and Cloud Services, see **paragraph 5.3**, no later than end of Fiscal Year (FY) 2018 (FY18) according to DoD guidance. Specific procedures for Application Hosting are in MPTO 00-33A-1113, *AFIN Server/Storage Management and Application Hosting.*

**5.2.7. User Assistant.** User Assistant services are established as the personnel, activities, methods, processes, procedures, capabilities, tools, and resources providing an interface to AFIN users for customer service functions, including service incident/problem reporting, IT service requests, service incident prioritization, operational impact reporting, and escalation to mission/functional unique application help desks. The primary AFIN organization designated for user assistance is the AF ESD. Specific Procedures are in the MPTO 00-33A-1112, *Air Force Network Enterprise Service Desk Service Incident Management.*

**5.2.8. Directory Services.** Directory Services are established as the activities, methods, processes, procedures, capabilities, tools, and resources that provide, operate, and maintain a global directory of AFIN users, objects, and resources. Directory services include appropriate identity and attribute information, allowing effective enterprise-wide identity management, authentication, and authorization to AFIN resources. Directory

Services are sourced from and rely on a number of AF and DoD organizations for account management and data accuracy. Specific procedures for Directory Services will be in the *Directory Services MPTO.*

5.3. Common Computing Environments, Cloud Security Requirements and Cloud Services.

5.3.1. The DoD CIO Cloud Computing Strategy (2012) provides Federal and DoD mandates for cloud computing adoption and identifies the three major benefits as efficiency, agility, and innovation. The DoD Cloud Computing Goal is to *"implement cloud computing as the means to deliver the most innovative, efficient, and secure information and IT services in support of the Department's mission, anywhere, anytime, on any authorized device."*

5.3.2. Common computing environments authorized for hosting AF core enterprise services, applications, and systems are limited to DoD Data Center, and commercially provided cloud services.

5.3.3. Cloud computing supports the Common Computing Environment (CCE) and provides capabilities for IaaS, PaaS, SaaS.

5.3.3.1. Infrastructure as a Service (IaaS) - Virtualized systems operated on fundamental computing resources (e.g., processing, storage, and network) managed as a cloud service with the AF retaining control of operating systems, storage, and deployed applications.

5.3.3.2. Platform as a Service (PaaS) - A cloud computing platform providing operating systems, database systems, web servers, security, etc. for hosting of AF unique applications. The AF is only retaining control of the hosted unique application(s) and not the operating systems, database systems, web servers, security, etc.

5.3.3.3. Software as a Service (SaaS) - All aspects of standard applications are provided as a cloud service to the AF. The AF does not retain control over the applications, platform or infrastructure.

5.3.4. DoD Security Requirements Guide (SRG) is security requirements applicable to a given technology family, product category, or an organization in general. Compliance with the SRG is a requirement and Mission Owners must comply with the requirements of the SRG for any commercial cloud environment, including government and commercial hosted cloud services. The SRG can be found at URL: **http://iase.disa.mil/cloud_security/Pages/index.aspx**.

5.3.4.1. Deleted.

5.3.4.2. Deleted.

5.3.4.3. Deleted.

5.3.5. Applications relocating to an approved DoD hosting environment must be vetted through the AF Application Rationalization process (see Figure 3). The AF application rationalization process is a four phase process that drives application reductions and data center closures to meet DoD goals. (2012 National Defense Authorization Act, section 2867, paragraph a.3.b.1.v).

5.3.5.1. Phase one of the AF Application Rationalization process (application discovery) requires the identification of applications residing on bases across the AF. Applications discovered by MAJCOMs, Forward Operating Agencies (FOAs), Direct Reporting Units (DRUs), Program Element Offices (PEOs), Mission Area Owners, and application owners must be registered to Enterprise Information Technology Data Repository (EITDR).

5.3.5.2. During the second phase (mid-level governance) MAJCOMs, FOAs, DRUs, PEOs, Mission Area Owners, and application owners identify the planned DoD hosting environment for their applications, submit their application disposition listings to SAF/CIO A6 to be included on the AF Application Disposition Listing, and present individual disposition listing(s) to the Information Technology Governance Executive Group and Board (ITGEG/B) for review and waiver approval.

5.3.5.3. In phase three (senior level governance) the ITGEG/B reviews MAJCOM, FOA, DRU, PEO or application owner migration plans and application hosting locations (application disposition listings) and approves waivers as required. MAJCOM, FOA, DRU, PEO and Functional application disposition listings will be combined to create the Air Force Application Disposition Listing.

5.3.5.4. Phase four (disposition) involves the movement of applications to a DoD approved hosting environment (e.g. IPN, CDC or MilCloud, SPPN, TPN, or the Commercial Cloud). Applications will be dispositioned and migrated per the AF Application Migration Execution Framework (see Figure 4) and the AF Application Migration Process (see Figure 5). The AF Application Rationalization Process, the AF Application Migration Execution Framework, the AF Application Migration Flowchart, and supplemental application migration documentation, can be found on the USAF Application Migration Website at URL: .

**Figure 3.  Air Force Application Rationalization Process.**

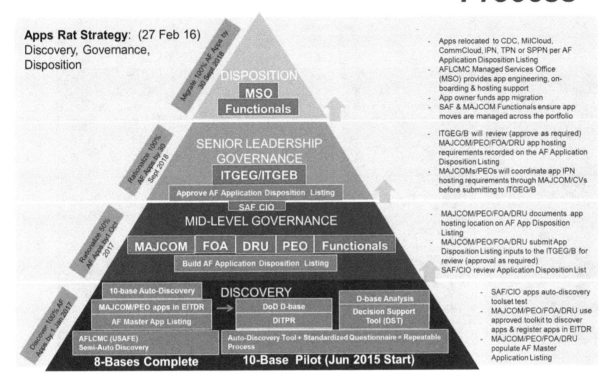

**Figure 4.  Air Force Application Migration Execution Framework.**

# Application Rationalization &
# Migration Execution Framework

Communication

Governance

Metrics

| Conduct Discovery | Perform Assessment and Analysis | Conduct Planning | Migrate Application |
|---|---|---|---|
| • Gather Application Data<br>  ▪ EITDR<br>  ▪ Installations<br>  ▪ Joint Bases<br>  ▪ Scans<br>  ▪ Data Calls<br><br>• Characterize Application Data | • Determine Assessment to Conduct<br><br>• Bin Data to Support Assessment<br><br>• Analyze Selected Criteria<br>  ▪ Functional<br>  ▪ Engineering<br>  ▪ Financial<br>  ▪ Cost Estimates<br>  ▪ Security<br><br>• Develop Proposed Disposition | • Conduct Deep Dive Engineering<br>• Programmatic Review<br>  ▪ Analyze Contracts<br>  ▪ Security Planning<br>  ▪ T&E Planning<br>  ▪ Compliance Planning<br>  ▪ Ops & Sustainment Planning<br>• Conduct Business Case Analysis<br>• Coordinate Funding<br>• Review, Approval, and Governance of disposition | • Conduct On-Boarding<br><br>• Coordinate Disposition<br><br>• Perform Acquisition<br><br>• Manage Sustainment<br><br>• Execute Application Disposition |
| Master Application Listing (EITDR) | Proposed Disposition | Approved Disposition Listing | Movement of Application to the To Be State |

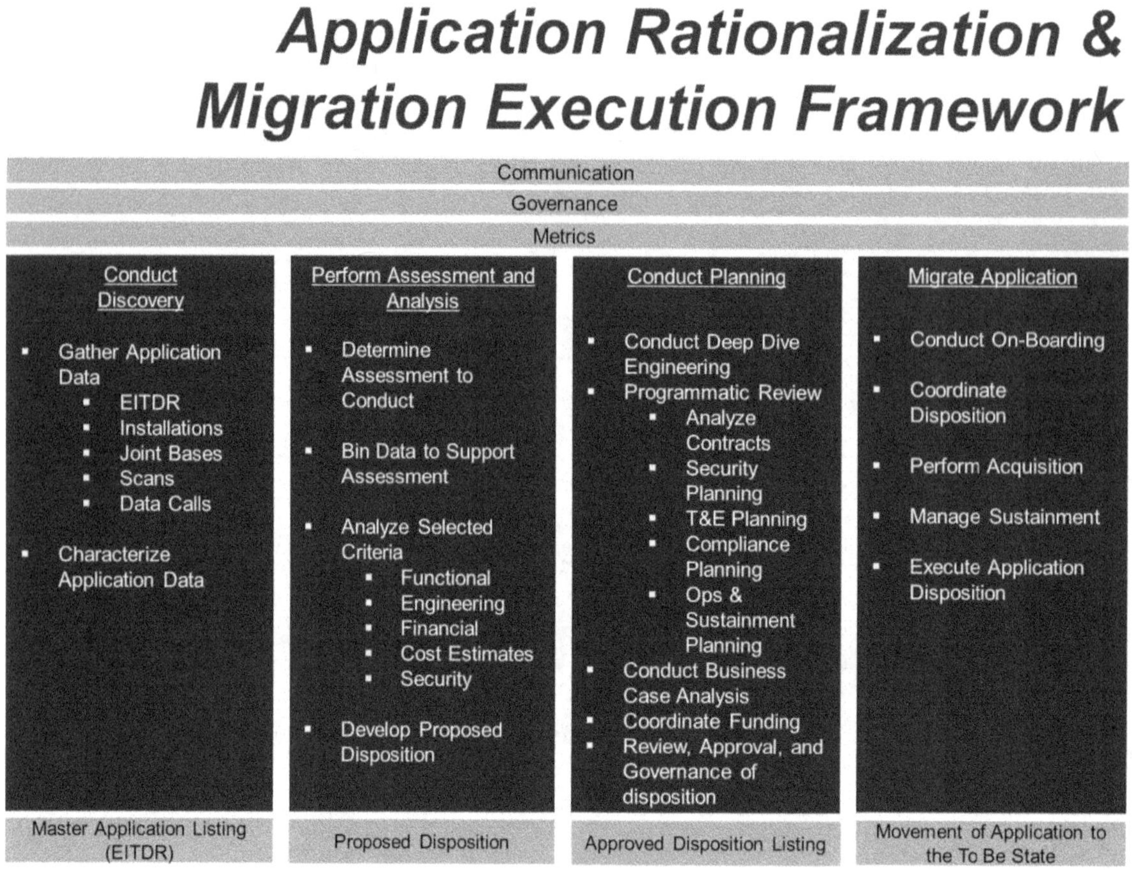

**Figure 5.  Air Force Application Migration Process Flowchart (DISCOVERY).**

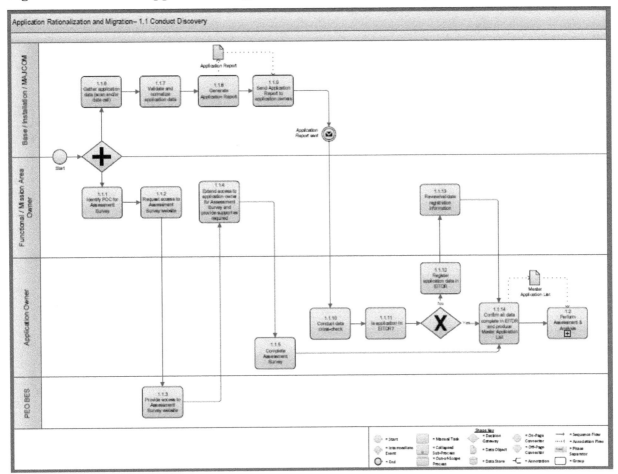

*Note: This flowchart and a narrative for each step in DISCOVERY is provided at URL: https://intelshare.intelink.gov/sites/afcce/SitePages/Home.aspx (click: Application Management then Application Rationalization).

**Figure 5.1.  Air Force Application Migration Process Flowchart (ASSESSMENT & ANALYSIS).**

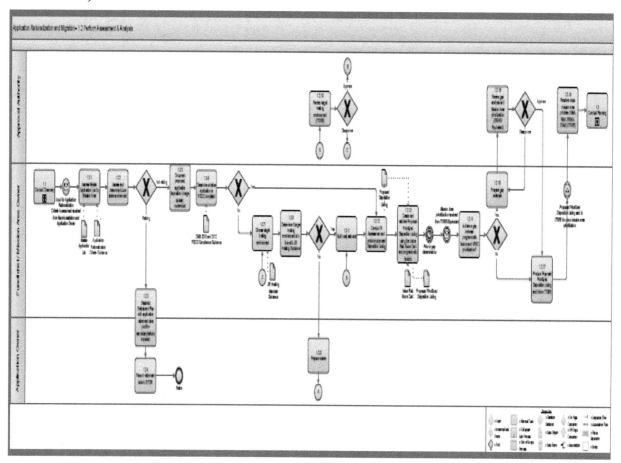

*Note: This flowchart and a narrative for each step in ASSESSMENT & ANALYSIS is provided at URL: https://intelshare.intelink.gov/sites/afcce/SitePages/Home.aspx (click: Application Management then Application Rationalization).

**Figure 5.2.   Air Force Application Migration Process Flowchart (CONDUCT PLANNING).**

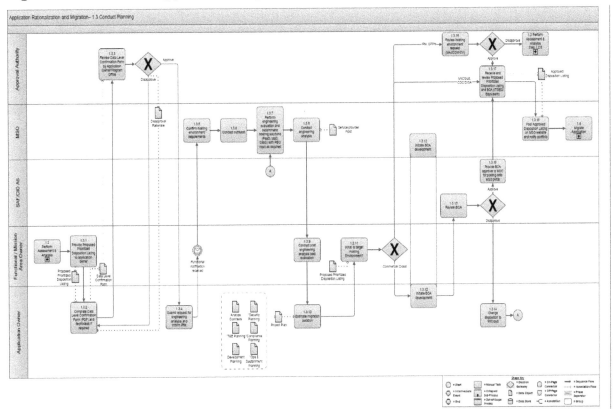

\*Note: This flowchart and a narrative for each step in CONDUCT PLANNING is provided at URL: https://intelshare.intelink.gov/sites/afcce/SitePages/Home.aspx (click: Application Management then Application Rationalization).

**Figure 5.3.  Air Force Application Migration Process Flowchart (MIGRATE APPLICATION).**

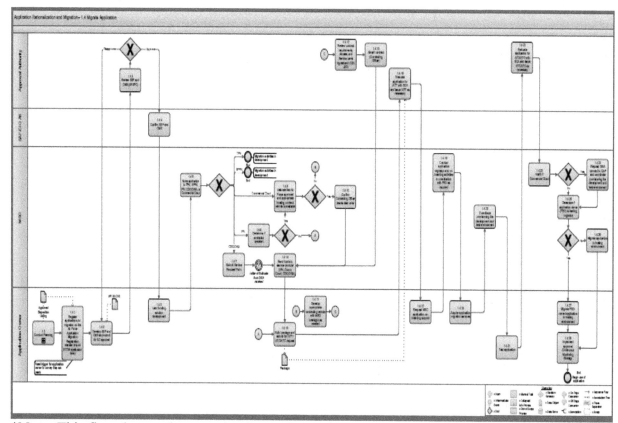

*Note: This flowchart and a narrative for each step in MIGRATE APPLICATION is provided at URL: https://intelshare.intelink.gov/sites/afcce/SitePages/Home.aspx (click: Application Management then Application Rationalization).

5.3.6. Organizations will maintain responsibility for their application and capabilities built on a cloud service and/or identified as a government responsibility in any applicable documentation for cybersecurity or approvals to operate for the cloud service.

5.3.6.1. Maintain AFIN networthiness by complying with AF AO (previously known as DAA) direction for executing secure operations functions within their operated portions of the AFIN extending to cloud services.

5.3.6.2. Ensure Air Force Information Technology (IT) utilizing cloud computing services follow the DoD Provisional Authorization process and receive Assessment and Authorization from the AF AO or designated Functional AO according to AFI 33-210, The Risk Management Framework (RMF) for Air Force Information Technology (IT). The RMF will utilize security control inheritance for security controls provided by the cloud service.

5.3.6.3. Deleted.

5.3.6.4. Web servers, services, applications, or capabilities for processing non-public information to be hosted on commercial servers or services (including cloud computing services) outside of military or government cybersecurity boundaries requires DoD Provisional Authorization and AF AO approval for use regardless of applicability of C&A requirements.

5.3.7. All Air Force data must be located on DoD or other USG premises or in an approved (having an appropriate PATO or ATO for its data level) government or commercial data center within the United States.

5.4. **Application Support Services.** Application Support Services should be provided by the Common Computing Environments. Application Support Services are the middleware and common services which enable cross-community of interest (COI) sharing of information and capabilities (exposure services, metadata repositories, mediation/translation, etc.). Application Support Services provide a set of tools, capabilities, processes, and methodologies to support enablement of a Service Oriented Architecture (SOA) for the AF and DoD enterprises.

5.4.1. **Mediation.** Mediation services are established as data aggregation, correlation, or transformation processing; data translation or fusion; negotiation services (brokering, trading and auctioning services); subscription and publication services, and workflow coordination services. Typically, mediation services intercept and modify messages that are passed between existing services (providers) and clients (requesters).

5.4.2. **Metadata.** Metadata is descriptive information about a particular data set, object, or resource, including how it is formatted, and when and by whom it was collected. Metadata services are established as procedures, guidelines, and methods for effective data planning, analysis, standards, modeling, configuration management, storage, retrieval, protection, validation, and documentation of metadata. Metadata will follow the DoD Metadata specification according to DoDI 8410.03. Although metadata most commonly refers to web resources, it can be about either physical or electronic resources.

5.4.3. **Exposure.** Exposure services are established as procedures, guidelines, and methods for making web services visible and discoverable. This exposure or visibility allows web services to be discovered or searched using service registries. Once web services are exposed and discovered or searched, a data or service consumer (person or machine user) can determine if the service/data is viable for consumption and use.

5.4.4. **Presentation.** Presentation services are established as the presentation layer for user access to an application. The presentation layer of an application can vary from a simple Web-based front end to a heavy client that has the user interface.

5.4.5. **Middleware.** Middleware services are established as the computer software that connects software components or people and their applications. The software consists of a set of services that allows multiple processes running on one or more machines to interact. This technology evolved to provide for interoperability in support of the move to coherent distributed architectures, which are most often used to support and simplify complex distributed applications. It includes web servers, application servers, and similar tools that support application development and delivery. Middleware is especially integral to modern information technology based on eXtensible Markup Language (XML), Simple Object Access Protocol (SOAP), Web Services, and Service Oriented Architecture (SOA).

5.4.6. **Enterprise Service Bus (ESB).** The Enterprise Service Bus is established as the construct for a standards-based integration platform that combines messaging, web services, data transformation, and intelligent routing to reliably connect and coordinate interactions of significant numbers of diverse applications across extended enterprises with transactional integrity. ESB integration fabric infrastructure shall include highly distributed, scalable service containers; event-driven change invocation; centralized management of distributed integration configurations; diverse client connectivity and support for multiple protocols; seamless, dynamic routing of data across physical deployment boundaries; unified security and access control model; distributed configuration and caching of deployment resources, such as Extensible Stylesheet Language Transformations (XSLT) documents and routing rules; scriptable and declarative environment.

5.5. **Mission/Functional Unique Applications (MFUAs).** Mission and Functional-Unique Applications are IT applications and/or systems which provide a mission-specific capability to one or more communities of interest, funded and managed by the requirements' owners. MFUAs rely on services from AF ITSM, Enterprise Core Services, and Application Support Services to function. Owners of MFUAs must use the information within this AFI and corresponding MPTOs to ensure their systems can efficiently interface with and leverage all applicable AF IT Services. MFUAs will adhere to applicable Baseline standards in accordance with **paragraph 6** and AFPD 33-4. MAJCOMs are responsible for managing and sustaining MAJCOM-unique systems. MFUA owners are responsible for reporting information, cost, plans, and status of applications to their respective MAJCOMs, SAF CIO, and Cyber CFL when requested.

6. **AFIN Baseline Management.** The Target, Implementation, and Operational Baselines address the technical standards, protocols and guidance to establish a consistent environment for IT capability engineering, development, deployment and support, see AFPD 33-4 for more information. The Baselines are prescriptive and include those things required to ensure a repeatable and predictable process by which to develop and deploy IT capabilities and of the infrastructure on which they operate. The Baselines apply to both AF-controlled portions of the NIPRNET and SIPRNET environments. Future technical standards, protocols, guidelines, and implementation constraints are provided by the Target Baseline. Selected products and their informed/allowed configurations are provided by the Implementation Baseline. Currently operational AF IT Services and their usage are provided by the Operational Baseline.

6.1. **HAF/SAF IT/Cyberspace Operational Baseline Modification Process.** Applies to new to the customer requirements.

6.1.1. The HAF/SAF customer shall coordinate the requirement with the appropriate AFSPC functional directorate. That AFSPC functional directorate shall work with the AFSPC A5/8 and the AFSPC A2/3/6 to determine if the customer request falls under the AF Cyberspace Infrastructure Planning System (CIPS) process or the Joint Capabilities Integration and Development System (JCIDS) process.

6.1.2. The customer enters a CIPS requirement into the CIPS Program for processing and the implementation is negotiated between the customer and implementing organizations.

6.1.3. If it is determined that the customer requirement falls under the JCIDS process the requirement is further refined between the AFSPC A5/8 and the HAF/A5.

6.1.4. The Information Dominance Flight Plan provides the strategic framework to articulate the cyber challenges faced by the Air Force as well as specific actions for moving forward across all Air Force core functional areas. The plan guides the efforts of the future Enterprise Architecture as well as the systematic alignment of resources across all Air Force Components. The strategic framework shapes the Portfolio Management and Capital Planning and Investment Control Process that is addressed in AFI 33-141. As such, any IT solutions requested as a result of these AFIs or this AFGM must be aligned to the goals of this strategic framework. This Flight Plan may be found at http://www.safcioa6.af.mil/.

**Figure 6.  HAF/SAF IT/Cyberspace Operational Baseline Modification Process.**

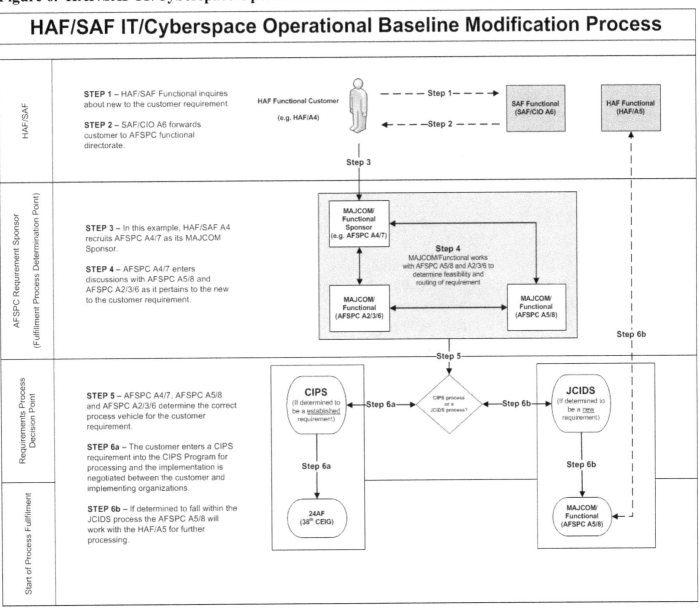

**7. Operation of AF IT Services within the AFIN.**

7.1. **Command and Control (C2) of the AFIN.** C2 of the AFIN is conducted to operate, secure, defend, maintain, and control the AFIN for the purposes of DoDIN Operations and Defensive Cyberspace Operations (DCO).

7.1.1. Operational type orders for C2 of the AFIN are defined and issued according to AFI 10-1701.

7.1.2. Operational type orders, AF TCTOs, and TCNOs issued for C2 of the AFIN take precedence over TOs, MPTOs, and TCTOs issued by PMOs, SPOs, and other organizations directing the standard operation and maintenance of the AFIN.

7.2. **Technical Orders (TOs).** The purpose of the Air Force Technical Order (TO) system in supporting AF IT Service Management is to provide clear and concise instructions for safe and reliable operation, inspection and maintenance of centrally acquired and managed AF systems and commodities.

7.2.1. Technical publications are essential for the proper function of AFIN Operations and to provide the operations activity with accurate information. Technical publications include TOs, MPTOs, commercial manuals, and specialized publications.

7.2.2. Technical publications for AF IT Service Management are developed and verified according to AFI 63-101, TO 00-5-1, *AF Technical Order System,* and TO 00-5-3, *AF Technical Order Life Cycle Management.*

7.2.3. All organizations supporting AF IT Service Management order TOs following procedures in TO 00-5-1.

7.2.4. Report any errors, contradictions, or procedures requiring clarification, by following procedures in TO 00-5-1 on preparing AFTO Form 22, *Technical Manual (TM) Change Recommendation and Reply.*

7.2.5. Compliance with AF IT Service Management TOs is mandatory, except as explained in TO 00-5-1.

7.3. **Method and Procedure Technical Orders (MPTOs).** Air Force 00-series MPTOs are procedure-oriented and provide general methods and procedures standardizing processes across the AF and are used to standardize AF IT Service Management. MPTOs are available for ordering through the Enhanced Technical Information Management System (ETIMS) application on the AF Portal, per TO 00-5-1. Contact unit Technical Order Distribution Office (TODO) for assistance.

7.3.1. AF IT Service Management MPTOs standardize AFIN ITSM processes and procedures and may integrate the operation of individual systems under AF IT Services. A full list of MPTOs directed by this AFI is located within **Attachment 1**.

7.3.2. TOs published for specific systems take precedence over AF IT Services MPTOs.

7.4. **Time Compliance Technical Orders (TCTOs).** TCTOs document all permanent modifications, update changes and retrofit changes to standard Air Force systems and commodities.

7.4.1. TCTOs are managed and issued according to TO 00-5-15, *Air Force Time Compliance Technical Order Process.*

7.4.2. TCTOs are military orders issued by order of the SECAF and as such, shall be complied with as specified in the TCTO.

**7.5. Time Compliance Network Orders (TCNOs).** TCNOs are downward-directed security or vulnerability-related orders issued by the AF.

7.5.1. TCNOs are generated internally to the AF or in response to an Information Assurance Vulnerability Alert (IAVA) or Information Assurance Vulnerability Bulletin (IAVB) to direct the implementation of an operational or security vulnerability risk mitigation procedure or fix action (countermeasure).

7.5.2. TCNOs are managed and issued according to MPTO 00-33A-1109, *Vulnerability Management* and under the authority of AFI 10-1701.

**7.6. One AF-One Network.** The lead command for Cyberspace Operations directs the operation, maintenance, configuration, and control of AF network infrastructure with the goal and objective of providing a single network for the AF that is managed, commanded/controlled, and fully compatible with a seamless DoD network.

7.6.1. Core Data Center (CDC):

7.6.1.1. CDCs are highly capable, highly resilient data centers providing standardized hosting and storage services to the enterprise within the Single Security Architecture (SSA) now being implemented.

7.6.1.2. CDCs also enable a significant reduction in the total number of DoD data centers by serving as consolidation points for computing and storage services currently hosted across hundreds of Component Facilities in accordance with DoD CIO memorandum, *Department of Defense Joint Information Environment: Continental United States Core Data Centers and Application and System Migration,* 11 July, 2013.

7.6.1.3. Deleted.

7.6.2. 2 Deleted.

7.6.2.1. An APC is a facility which provides enterprise and regional computing and data centers supporting Enterprise Core Services.

7.6.2.2. Per DoD CIO guidance (1 Nov 2012), APCs will either convert to IPNs or close as approved by the ITGEB. APCs will meet DoD standards for facility and network infrastructure, security, technology and operations, and adhere to DoD enterprise governance, (T-0).

7.6.2.3. If not designated as a CDC, organizations will plan for transition of systems to a designated CDC under JIE construct, (T-0).

7.6.3. Installation Processing Node (IPN):

7.6.3.1. An IPN is a facility which provides a consolidated base-level computing and data processing node for all NIPRNET and SIPRNET systems which are unable to be hosted at a DoD enterprise-level data center (e.g., CDC) based upon validated Disconnected, Intermittent, Limited (DIL) requirements.

7.6.3.2. IPNs will be designated by the ITGEB when sites are approved as an AF data center, (T-0).

7.6.3.3. IPNs will provide 24-hour, 7-days a week on-site hardware maintenance, environmental control, space utilization, and physical security of the base-level processing node.

7.6.3.4. IPNs will conform to the AF's implementation of FDCCI.

7.6.4. **Installation Services Node (ISN):**

7.6.4.1. An ISN is the required localized equipment necessary to provide the minimum basic functionality to an installation should it become disconnected from the enterprise.

7.6.4.2. Potential services include anomaly detection, audit functions, Active Directory (AD), DNS, Assured Compliance Assessment Solution (ACAS), Host Based Security System (HBSS), and print services. In addition, ISNs may also host unified capabilities (UC) that must remain on the Installation to enable emergency services even when the connection is interrupted.

7.6.5. Special Purpose Processing Node (SPPN):

7.6.5.1. A SPPN is a facility which provides a fixed processing node supporting data servers and special purpose functions that cannot be supported by a IPN, CDC, or other DoD enterprise-level data center due to its association with mission specific infrastructure or equipment.

7.6.5.2. SPPNs will be designated by the ITGEB when sites are approved as an AF data center, (T-0).

7.6.5.3. SPPNs will be supported and maintained by the functional community of interest requiring the SPPN.

7.7. **Cybersecurity (previously known as Information Assurance[IA]).** All systems (e.g., centrally managed applications) will comply with AF Cybersecurity program guidance in AFI 33-200, *Information Assurance (IA) Management*, DOD Cybersecurity program guidance, and U.S. Strategic Command (USSTRATCOM) warning and tactical directives/orders (e.g., Information Assurance Vulnerability Management (IAVM) program, security incident handling program, and other responsibilities outlined in CJCSI 6510.01, *Information Assurance (IA) and Support to Computer Network Defense (CND)*).

7.7.1. Authorizing Official (AO) (previously known as Designated Accrediting Authority [DAA]) Approval. All systems must receive accreditation and authorization to operate by the appropriate AO prior to operational use according to AFI 33-210.

7.7.2. Reciprocity, Reuse, and Inheritance.   The AF recognizes and fully supports reciprocity and reuse according to AFI 33-210.   In order to minimize certification and accreditation (C&A) workload and paperwork, AOs and Information Systems Security Manager (ISSM), (previously known as IAM) will fully embrace and support inheritance in which AF IT Services and mission/functional unique applications inherit security controls and other Cybersecurity attributes as reuse from other associated services, hosting environments, security solution, etc., as appropriate.  Cybersecurity policy takes precedence if Cybersecurity policy provides specific guidance for inheritance in the future.

**7.8. Commercial Internet Service Provider (ISP) Connections and DoDIN Wavier Process.**

7.8.1. A DoDIN Waiver (previously known as DOD GIG Waiver) is required for any internet connection not utilizing the DoDIN infrastructure/transport services to allow a direct unfettered and non-attributable connection to the public Internet in the performance of DoD/AF missions.  For more information about DoDIN Waivers and commercial ISPs refer to AFI 33-200.    The commercial ISP connection cannot be connected to the NIPRNET (Use of an approved hardware/software secure tunnel across a commercial ISP circuit to connect to the NIPRNET/DoDIN is allowed).

7.8.2. **Quality-of-Life (QoL) Internet Services**. The QoL Internet Services may be established for "patron" activities such as the Family Support Center, library, dormitories, medical treatment facilities, lodging, and other services facilities.

> 7.8.2.1. For Morale, Welfare and Recreation (MWR) Category A, B, and C activities, refer to AFI 65-106, *Appropriated Fund Support of Morale, Welfare, and Recreation (MWR) and Nonappropriated Fund Instrumentalities (NAFIS)*.

> 7.8.2.2. For QoL internet access in Dormitories, refer to AFI 32-6005, *Unaccompanied Housing Management*.

> 7.8.2.3. These systems shall not be connected to the base network/NIPRNET with the privileges of ".mil" registered users.

> 7.8.2.4. Official business activities and administrative offices in these QoL locations may require and are authorized NIPRNET connectivity through the base network according to AFI 65-106.   Refer to AFI 65-106 for the funding of NIPRNET installation, sustainment and management in MWR facilities.

> 7.8.2.5. Certification and Accreditation (C&A) is not required for QoL Internet Services.

> 7.8.2.6. Commercial ISPs used as Quality of Life (QoL) internet service for patrons are exempted from the DoDIN Waiver process.

7.8.3. Portions of the AF Services' mission must be conducted outside of the NIPRNET to comply with AF Cybersecurity policies.  Although some patron-based activities are supported by the QoL networks, the vast majority of services user base, systems support organizations, and management activities are not permitted to operate on the NIPRNET, but still require identity authentication.  AFPC Services Directorate is authorized to connect to commercial ISP nodes to support and manage the Services NAFIS that are not allowed on the NIPRNET according to AFI 65-106.

7.8.4. DOD Dependent Schools and Base Education Offices.   Only government personnel and/or government contractors are authorized Internet access through NIPRNET.   Internet access for classroom education or civilian education institutions must be through a commercial ISP (or DISA's Private ISP when available) and cannot be connected to the NIPRNET.

7.8.5. Headquarters Air Education and Training Command (HQ AETC) and the United States Air Force Academy (USAFA).   HQ AETC and USAFA require academic networks that provide students, faculty, and staff IT services that are not available on the AFNET (i.e., conduct research and scientific collaborations).   Consequently, HQ AETC and USAFA are authorized to operate networks specifically designed to IT enable their education and training missions.

7.8.6. Geographically Separated Unit (GSU).   The GSU owning MAJCOM is required to provide funding to the supporting base, MAJCOM or AFSPC for any network circuit(s) required for the GSU connectivity.   GSUs will comply with all policies and directives of their servicing AFIN Operations activities including the CFP supporting their network circuit.

7.8.7. When available, DISA's Private ISP Service (through AF Guest Network) will be the default method for obtaining direct, unfettered, and non-attributable access to the public Internet in the performance of DoD/AF missions (not MWR or QoL).   DISA Private ISP connections will be exempt from the DoDIN Waiver requirements as DISA is the service provider.

7.9. **Sharing Data, Information, and Information Technology Services.** All Authoritative Data Sources (ADSs) should be exposed as Data-as-a-Service (DaaS).

7.9.1. Data shall remain as closely controlled as possible by the ADS steward to ensure its currency and accuracy.

7.9.2. Systems and services shall reference ADSs rather than duplicate or provision external source data for anything beyond short-term consumption or proxying for performance or security reasons.

7.9.3. Sharing of data, information, and IT services shall be managed according to DoDD 8320.02.

7.9.4. Data authentication and control shall be managed according to DoDI 8520.03, *Identity Authentication for Information Systems.*

7.10. **Service Level Agreements (SLA), Memorandums of Agreement (MOA), Memorandums of Understanding (MOU).** SLAs will be established by AFSPC for AF IT Services to define division of responsibilities for network operations and services to minimize duplication of effort between organizations.

7.10.1. Enterprise service SLAs will be established for ESUs and the AF ESD with approval by the ITGEB.

7.10.2. An MOA, MOU, or Operational Level Agreement (OLA) will be established as appropriate for organizations or users whose network support requirements exceed the standards of an enterprise service SLA.

7.10.3. Whenever possible, SLAs will identify the minimum levels of support required by the users rather than acceptable failure rates (uptime rates as opposed to downtime rates). SLAs will also describe the prioritization of systems and services to meet mission assurance requirements.

7.11. **AFIN Operations Training.** Refer to AFI 33-154, *Air Force On-The-Job Training Products for Cyberspace Support Enlisted Specialty Training* and MPTO 00-33A-1001, for policy and procedures for AFIN Operations training. Cyberspace Operations Training is covered under AFPD 10-17 and AFI 10-1703 Volume 1 *Cyberspace Operations Cyber Crew Training.*

WILLIAM J. BENDER, Lt Gen, USAF
Chief, Information Dominance and
Chief Information Officer

**Attachment 1**

**GLOSSARY OF REFERENCES AND SUPPORTING INFORMATION**

*References*

DOD5400.7-R_AFMAN33-302, *Freedom of Information Act Program*, 16 May 2016

National Defense Authorization Act (NDAA) Fiscal Year 2012, § 2867, *Data Servers and Centers*, 31 December 2011

CJCSI 6510.01, *Information Assurance (IA) and Support to Computer Network Defense (CND)*, 9 February 2011

CNSSI 4009, *National Information Assurance (IA) Glossary*, 26 April 2010

DoD 5012.02-STD, *Electronic Records Management Software Applications Design Criteria Standard*, 25 April, 2007

DoDD 8000.01, *Management of the Department of Defense Information Enterprise*, 10 February 2009

DoDI 5000.02, *Operation of the Defense Acquisition System*, 25 November 2013

DoDI 8100.04, *DoD Unified Capabilities (UC)*, 9 December 2010

DoDI 8320.02, *Sharing Data, Information, and Technology (IT) Services In The Department Of Defense*, 5 August 2013

DoDI 8410.01, *Internet Domain Name Use and Approval*, 14 April 2008

DoDI 8410.02, *NetOps for the Global Information Grid (GIG)*, 19 December 2008

DoDI 8410.03, *Network Management (NM)*, 29 August 2012

DoDI 8520.03, *Identity Authentication for Information Systems*, 13 May 2011

DoDI 8550.01, *DoD Internet Services and Internet-Based Capabilities*, 11 September 2012

DoD CIO Memo, *Approvals/Waivers for Obligation of Funds for Data Servers and Centers*, 26 June 2012

DoD CIO Memo, *Exemption for Obligation of funds for Data Servers and Data Centers Related to the High Performance Computing Modernization Program*, 25 January 2013

DoD CIO Memo, *Approvals/Waivers for Obligation of Funds for Data Servers and Centers*, 9 May 2013

DoD CIO Memo, *Department of Defense Joint Information Environment: Continental United States Core Data Centers and Application and System Migration*, 11 July 2013

AFI 33-364, *Records Disposition—Procedures and Responsibilities*, 9 April 2015

AFI 51-301, *Civil Litigation*, 20 JUNE 2002

AFPD 10-17, *Cyberspace Operations*, 31 July 2012

AFPD 33-1, *Cyberspace Support*, 9 August 2012

AFPD 33-2, *Information Assurance (IA) Program*, 3 August 2011

AFPD 33-3, *Information Management*, 8 September 2011

AFPD 33-4, *Information Technology Governance*, 17 January 2013

AFPD 33-5, *Warfighting Integration*, 11 January 2013

AFPD 63-1/20-1, *Integrated Life Cycle Management*, 3 July 2012

AFPD 71-1, *Criminal Investigations and Counterintelligence*, 6 January 2010

AFI 10-1701, *Command and Control (C2) of Cyberspace*, 5 March 2014

AFI 10-701, *Operations Security (OPSEC)*, 8 June 2011

AFI 10-710, *Information Operations Condition (INFOCON) (FOUO)*, 10 August 2006

AFI 33-141, *Air Force Information Technology Portfolio Management and IT Investment Review*, 23 December 2008

AFI 33-150, *Management of Cyberspace Support Activities*, 30 November 2011

AFI 33-154, *Air Force On-The-Job Training Products for Cyberspace Support Enlisted Specialty Training*, 1 May 2013

AFI 33-200, *Information Assurance (IA) Management*, 23 December 2008

AFI 33-210, *Air Force Certification and Accreditation Program (AFCAP)*, 23 December 2008

AFI 33-360, Publications and Forms Management, 25 September 2013

AFI 33-401, *Air Force Architecting*, 17 May 2011

AFI 35-102, *Security and Policy Review Process*, 20 October 2009

AFI 35-107, *Public Web Communications*, 21 October  2009

AFI 36-2640, *Executing Total Force Development*, 16 December 2008

AFI 63-101/20-101, *Integrated Life Cycle Management*, 7 March 2013

AFI 63-131, *Modification Program Management*, 19 March 2013

AFI 65-106, *Appropriated Fund Support of Morale, Welfare, and Recreation (MWR) and Nonappropriated Fund Instrumentalities (NAFIS)*, 6 May 2009

AFMAN 33-145, *Collaboration Services and Voice Systems Management*, 6 September 2012

AFMAN 33-152, *User Responsibilities and Guidance for Information Systems*, 1 June 2012

AFMAN 33-153, *IT Asset Management*, 19 March 2014

AFMAN 33-363, *Management of Records*, 1 March 2008

Air Force Performance Plan for Reduction of Resources Required for Data Servers and Centers, 31 January 2012

TO 00-5-1, *AF Technical Order System*

TO 00-5-3, *AF Technical Order Life Cycle Management*

TO 00-5-15, *Air Force Time Compliance Technical Order Process*

MPTO 00-33A-1001 *General Cyberspace Support Activities Management Procedures and Practice Requirements*

MPTO 00-33A-1100, *AF-GIG Operational Change Management Process*

MPTO 00-33A-1106, *Air Force Information Network (AFIN) Network Management*

MPTO 00-33A-1108, AFIN *Voice Systems Management*

MPTO 00-33A-1109, *Vulnerability Management*

MPTO 00-33A-1112, *Air Force Network Enterprise Service Desk Service Incident Management*

MPTO 00-33A-1113, AFIN *Server/Storage Management and Application Hosting*

MPTO 00-33A-1114, AFIN *Problem Management*

MPTO 00-33A-XXXX, *Directory Services*

MPTO 00-33A-XXXX, *Mission Assurance and Situational Awareness*

MPTO 00-33A-XXXX, *Discovery and Information Management*

MPTO 00-33A-XXXX, *End-to-End Performance Monitoring*

MPTO 00-33B-5007, *Security Incident Management for Information Systems*

MPTO 00-33D-2002, *Engineering Installation and Cyberspace Readiness Activities Management*

MPTO 00-33D-3003, *Managing the Cyberspace Infrastructure with the Cyberspace Infrastructure Planning System*

**Prescribed Forms**

No prescribed forms are implemented by this publication.

**Adopted Forms**

AFTO Form 22, *Technical Manual (TM) Change Recommendation and Reply*

AFTO Form 265, *Request For Change*

AF Form 847, *Recommendation for Change of Publication*

AF Form 1067, *Modification Proposal.*

**Abbreviations and Acronyms**

**ADS**—Authoritative Data Source

**AETC**—Air Education and Training Command

**AF—GIG**—Air Force-Global Information Grid

**AF CEITB**—Air Force Consolidated Enterprise Information Technology Baseline

**AFCAP**—Air Force Certification and Accreditation Program

**AFECMO**—Air Force Enterprise Configuration Management Office

**AF ESD**—Air Force Enterprise Service Desk

**AFFOR**—Air Force Forces

**AFI**—Air Force Instruction

**AFIN**—Air Force Information Networks

**AFMAN**—Air Force Manual

**AFMC**—Air Force Material Command

**AFNET**—Air Force Network

**AFNIC**—Air Force Network Integration Center

**AFPD**—Air Force Policy Directive

**AFR**—Air Force Reserves

**AFSPC**—Air Force Space Command

**AIRCOM**—Air Communications

**AIS**—Automated Information Systems

**ANG**—Air National Guard

**AO**—Authorizing Official (previously known as DAA)

**APC**—Area Processing Center

**ASI**—Authorized Service Interruptions

**C-NAF**—Component Number Air Force

**C&A**—Certification and Accreditation

**C2**—Command and Control

**C3I&N**—Command, Control, Communications, Intelligence and Networks

**CCB**—Configuration Control Board

**CCMD**—Combatant Command

**CDC**—Core Data Center

**CEIG**—Cyberspace Engineering Installation Group

**CFL**—Core Function Lead

**CFP**—Communications Focal Point

**CI**—Counter Intelligence

**CIO**—Chief Information Officer

**CIPS**—Cyberspace Infrastructure Planning System

**CND**—Computer Network Defense

**COI**—Community of Interest

**COOP**—Continuity of Operations Plan

**COTS**—Commercial of the Shelf

**CSAF**—Chief of Staff of the Air Force

**CSI**—Cyber Systems Integrator

**DaaS**—Data-as-a-Service

**DAA**—Designated Accrediting Authority (now refered to as AO)

**DCO**—Defensive Cyberspace Operations

**DESMF**—Defense Enterprise Service Management Framework

**DIL**—Disconnected, Intermittent, Limited

**DIMA**—Defense Intelligence Mission Area

**DISA**—Defense Information Systems Agency

**DMZ**—Demilitarized Zone

**DNI**—Director of National Intelligence

**DNS**—Domain Name Service

**DoD**—Department of Defense

**DoDD**—Department of Defense Directive

**DoDI**—Department of Defense Instruction

**DoDIN**—Department of Defense Information Networks

**DOTMLPF**—Doctrine, Organization, Training, Material, Leadership & Education, Personnel & Facilities

**DRU**—Direct Reporting Unit

**DSCC**—Defense Server Core Configuration

**EA**—Enterprise Architecture

**ECSB**—Enterprise Cloud Service Broker

**EITSM**—Enterprise Information Technology Service Manager

**ESB**—Enterprise Service Bus

**ESD**—Enterprise Service Desk

**ESI**—Enterprise Software Initiative

**ESU**—Enterprise Services Unit

**FOA**—Field Operating Agency

**FSA**—Functional System Administrator

**GIG**—Global Information Grid

**GSU**—Geographically Separated Unit

**HQ**—Headquarters

**IA**—Information Assurance

**IaaS**—Infrastructure-as-a Service

**IAVA**—Information Assurance Vulnerability Alert

**IAVB**—Information Assurance Vulnerability Bulletin

**IAVM**—Information Assurance Vulnerability Management

**IbC**—Internet-based Capabilities

**IB**—Implementation Baseline

**IC**—Intelligence Community

**ILCM**—Integrated Life Cycle Management

**IMDS**—Integrated Maintenance Data System

**INFOCON**—Information Condition

**I-NOSC**—Integrated Network Operations and Security Center

**IP**—Internet Protocol

**IPN**—Installation Processing Node

**IS**—Information Systems

**ISN**—Installation Services Node

**IT**—Information Technology

**ITGEB**—IT Governance Executive Board

**ITIL**—Information Technology Infrastructure Library

**ITS**—Information Transport System

**ITSM**—Information Technology Service Management

**JIE**—Joint Information Environment

**JTF**—Joint Task Force

**KO**—Knowledge Operations

**MAJCOM**—Major Command

**M/ACCC**—MAJCOM/Air Force Forces Command Coordination Center

**MFUA**—Mission/Functional Unique Applications

**MOA**—Memorandum of Agreement

**MOU**—Memorandum of Understanding

**MPA**—Military Personnel Appropriation

**MPTO**—Methods and Procedures Technical Order

**MWR**—Morale, Welfare, and Recreation

**NAF**—Numbered Air Force

**NAFIS**—Non-Appropriated Fund Instrumentalities

**NetD**—Network Defense

**NetOps**—Network Operations

**NIPRNET**—Non-Secure Internet Protocol Router Network

**NM**—Network Management

**NOS**—Network Operations Squadron

**NS**—Name Server

**NSS**—National Security System

**OLA**—Operational Level Agreement

**PA**—Public Affairs

**PAO**—Public Affairs Officer

**OPR**—Office of Primary Responsibility

**PaaS**—Platform-as-a-Service

**PBNM**—Policy Based Network Management

**PEO**—Program Executive Office

**PMO**—Program Management Office

**QoL**—Quality of Life

**QoS**—Quality of Service

**RDS**—Records Disposition Schedule

**SAF**—Secretary of the Air Force

**SAP**—Special Access Program

**SCCM**—Systems Center Configuration Manager

**SCI**—Sensitive Compartmented Information

**SDC**—Standard Desktop Configuration

**SECAF**—Secretary of the Air Force

**SDDP**—Service Development and Delivery Processes

**SINE**—Single Integrated Network Environment

**SIPRNET**—SECRET Internet Protocol Router Network

**SLA**—Service Level Agreement

**SOA**—Service Oriented Architecture

**SOAP**—Simple Object Access Protocol

**SPO**—System Program Office

**SPPN**—Special Purpose Processing Node

**T.O.**—Technical Order

**TB**—Target Baseline

**TCM**—Technical Content Management

**TCNO**—Time Compliance Network Order

**TCTO**—Time Compliance Technical Order

**TM**—Technical Manual

**UC**—Unified Capabilities

**USAF**—United States Air Force

**USAFA**—United States Air Force Academy

**USCYBERCOM**—United States Cyber Command

**VLAN**—Virtual Local Area Network

**VoIP**—Voice Over Internet Protocol

**XML**—Extensible Markup Language

**XSLT**—Extensible Stylesheet Language Transformation

*Terms*

**Air Force Information Networks (AFIN)**—The globally interconnected, end-to-end set of AF unique information capabilities, and associated processes for collecting, processing, storing, disseminating, and managing information on-demand to warfighters, policy makers, and support personnel, including owned and leased communications and computing systems and services, software (including applications), data, and security.

**AFIN Operations**— Operations to design, build, configure, secure, operate, maintain, and sustain AF networks to create and preserve information assurance on the AF information networks.

**AF IT Services**—The IT networks, systems, processes, and capabilities which enable the seamless, secure, and reliable exchange of information across the AFIN.

**Air Force Network (AFNET)**—The AF's underlying Non-Secure Internet Protocol Router Network (NIPRNET) that enables AF operational capabilities and lines of business.

**AFNET-S**— The AF's underlying Secret Internet Protocol Router Network that enables AF operational capabilities and lines of business.

**Authoritative Data Source (ADS)**—A source of data or information that is recognized by members of a Community Of Interest to be valid or trusted because it is considered to be highly reliable or accurate or is from an official publication or reference.

**Core Data Center**—The backbone of the JIE, CDCs are highly capable, highly resilient data centers providing standardized hosting and storage services to the enterprise within the Single

Security Architecture (SSA). CDCs also enable a significant reduction in the total number of DoD data centers by serving as consolidation points for computing and storage services currently hosted across hundreds of Component Facilities.  (DoD CIO memorandum, *Department of Defense Joint Information Environment:  Continental United States Core Data Centers and Application and System Migration*, 11 July 2013)

**Cyber Incident**—Actions taken through the use of computer networks that result in an actual or potentially adverse effect on an information system and/or the information residing therein. (CNSSI 4009)

**Cyberspace Operations**—The employment of cyber capabilities where the primary purpose is to achieve military objectives or effects in or through cyberspace. (AFPD 10-17)

**Data Center**—Accordingly, under the FDCCI, a data center is now defined as a closet, room, floor or building for the storage, management, and dissemination of data and information. Such a repository houses computer systems and associated components, such as database, application, and storage systems and data stores.' A data center generally includes redundant or backup power supplies, redundant data communications connections, environmental control (air conditioning, fire suppression, etc.) and special security devices housed in leased (including by cloud providers), owned, collocated, or stand-alone facilities. Under this revised definition, neither square footage nor Uptime Institute tier classifications are required to define a facility as a data center. (OMB memorandum, *Implementation Guidance for the Federal Data Center Consolidation Initiative (FDCCI)*, 19 March 2012)

**Department of Defense Information Network (DoDIN)**—The globally interconnected, end-to-end set of information capabilities, and associated processes for collecting, processing, storing, disseminating, and managing information on-demand to warfighters, policy makers, and support personnel, including owned and leased communications and computing systems and services, software (including applications), data, and security (formerly known as GIG). (JP 3-12)

**DoDIN Operations**—Operations to design, build, configure, secure, operate, maintain, and sustain Department of Defense networks to create and preserve information assurance on the Department of Defense information networks. (JP 3-12)

**Enterprise Core Services**—Standard IT capabilities available to all users on the AFIN. Enterprise Core Services support DoD Net-Centric strategies for data and services by enabling users to safeguard, compile, catalog, discover, cache, distribute, retrieve, and share data in a collaborative environment across the AF and DoD enterprises.

**Implementation Baseline**—The Implementation Baseline is the baseline of acquisition selected products and their informed/allowed configurations that implement the architecture, standards and protocols and guidelines specified in the Target Baseline.  The Implementation Baseline informs the Operational Baseline of the acquisition selected products and how they are to be configured to support deployment of user applications across the infrastructure topology.  The Implementation Baseline governs the implementation of the Development and Integration/Test environments (AFPD 33-4).

**Information Enviroment (IE)**—The aggregate of individuals, organizations, and systems that collect, process, disseminate, or act on information.  The information environment, which includes cyberspace, consists of three interrelated dimensions that continuously interact with individuals, organizations, and systems. These dimensions are the physical, informational, and cognitive. (JP 3-13 and Draft DoDI 8115.02)

**Information Processing Node**—A fixed DoD data center serving a single DoD installation and local area (installations physically or logically behind the network boundary) with local services that cannot (technically or economically) be provided from a CDC. There will be no more than one IPN per DoD installation but each IPN may have multiple enclaves to accommodate unique installation needs (e.g., Joint Bases)

**Information Technology**—Any equipment or interconnected system or subsystem of equipment that is used in the automatic acquisition, storage, manipulation, management, movement, control, display, switching, interchange, transmission, or reception of data or information by the executive agency. For purposes of the preceding sentence, equipment is used by an executive agency if the equipment is used by the executive agency directly or is used by a contractor under a contract with the executive agency which (i) requires the use of such equipment or (ii) requires the use, to a significant extent, of such equipment in the performance of a service or the furnishing of a product. The term information technology includes computers, ancillary equipment, software, firmware and similar procedures, services (including support services), and related resources. (CNSSI 4009)

**Infrastructure—as-a-Service (IaaS)**—Virtualized systems operated on fundamental computing resources (e.g., processing, storage, network) managed as a cloud service with the AF retaining control of operating systems, storage, and deployed applications.

**Installation Services Node (ISN)**—An Installation services node is the required localized equipment necessary to provide the minimum basic functionality to an installation should it become disconnected from the enterprise. Potential services include anomaly detection, audit functions, Active Directory (AD), DNS, Assured Compliance Assessment Solution (ACAS), Host Based Security System (HBSS), and print services. In addition ISNs may also host unified capabilities (UC) that must remain on the Installation to enable emergency services even when the connection is interrupted.

**Internet**—An informal global collection of government, military, commercial, and educational computer networks. The global collection of interconnected local, mid-level, and wide area networks that use IP as the network layer protocol.

**Internet-based Capabilities**—All public information capabilities or applications available across the Internet from locations not directly or indirectly controlled by DoD or the Federal government (i.e., locations not owned or operated by DoD or another Federal agency or by contractors or others on behalf of DoD or another Federal agency).

**Internet Service Provider**—A commercial entity providing data connectivity into the Internet.

**Joint Information Environment**—A secure joint information environment, comprised of shared information technology (IT) infrastructure, enterprise services, and a single security architecture to achieve full spectrum superiority, improve mission effectiveness, increase security and realize IT efficiencies. JIE is operated and managed per the Unified Command Plan (UCP) using enforceable standards, specifications, and common tactics, techniques, and procedures (TTPs).

**Operational Baseline**—The Operational Baseline is the set of components of the Implementation Baseline appropriately configured and deployed across the topology of the AFIN infrastructure that implements the architecture, standards and protocols and guidelines specified in the Target Baseline and provide the required warfighter capabilities and performance. It specifies the exact laydown and configurations of hardware and software within all facilities in the AF infrastructure topology.

**Platform—as-a-Service (PaaS)**—A cloud computing platform providing operating systems, database systems, web servers, security, etc. for hosting of AF unique applications.

**Security Incident**—An assessed occurrence that actually or potentially jeopardizes the confidentiality, integrity, or availability of an information system; or the information the system processes, stores, or transmits; or that constitutes a violation or imminent threat of violation of security policies, security procedures, or acceptable use policies. (CNSSI 4009 - *Security Incident refers to Incident*)

**Server**—A hardware platform (computer) that houses software providing service to other computers or programs to satisfy client requests and needs.

**Service Incident**—Any event which is not part of the standard operation of a service and which causes or may cause an interruption to, or a reduction in, the quality of that service. (ISO 20000 – *ITSM definition of Incident*) An unplanned interruption to an IT service or reduction in the quality of an IT service. Failure of a configuration item that has not yet affected service is also an incident – for example, failure of one disk from a mirror set. (ITIL Version 3 Service Operation)

**Service Oriented Architecture**—A set of principles and methodologies for designing and developing software in the form of interoperable services.

**Service Request**—A request from a user for information, or advice, or for a standard change or for access to an IT Service. For example to reset a password, or to provide standard IT Services for a new user. Service Requests are usually handled by a Service Desk, and do not require an request for change to be submitted. (ITIL Version 3 Service Operation)

**Software—as-a-Service (SaaS)**—All aspects of standard applications are provided as a cloud service to the AF.

**Special Purpose Processing Node (SPPN)**—A fixed data center supporting special purpose functions that cannot (technically or economically) be supported by CDCs or IPNs due to association with infrastructure or equipment (e.g., communication and networking, manufacturing, training, education, meteorology, medical, modeling & simulation, test ranges, etc.). No general purpose processing or general purpose storage can be provided by or through a SPPN. SPPNs do not have direct connection to the Global Information Grid (GIG); they must connect through a CDC or IPN. (DoD CIO memorandum, "Department of Defense Joint Information Environment: Continental United States Core Data Centers and Application and System Migration," 11 July, 2013)

**Target Baseline**—The Target Baseline specifies the standards, protocols, guidelines and implementation constraints for the future state of the AFIN infrastructure. It is used to inform the development of the Implementation Baseline. The Target Baseline is thoroughly documented and continually updated based upon emerging industry standards and the evolving AF enterprise architecture.

**Unified Capabilities (UC)**—The integration of voice, video, and/or data services delivered ubiquitously across a secure and highly available network infrastructure, independent of technology, to provide increased mission effectiveness to the warfighter and business communities. (DODI 8100.04)

**User**—The individual who operates the computer or uses application software.

# Cybersecurity Titles Published by 4<sup>th</sup> Watch Publishing Co.

**NIST SP 500-288** Specification for WS-Biometric Devices (WS-BD)
**NIST SP 500-291 V2** NIST Cloud Computing Standards Roadmap
**NIST SP 500-292** NIST Cloud Computing Reference Architecture
**NIST SP 500-293 V1 & V2** US Government Cloud Computing Technology Roadmap
**NIST SP 500-293 V3** US Government Cloud Computing Technology Roadmap
**NIST SP 500-299** NIST Cloud Computing Security Reference Architecture
**NIST SP 500-304** Data Format for the Interchange of Fingerprint, Facial & Other Biometric Information
**NIST SP 800-12 R1** An Introduction to Information Security
**NIST SP 800-16 R1** A Role-Based Model for Federal Information Technology/Cybersecurity Training
**NIST SP 800-18 R1** Developing Security Plans for Federal Information Systems
**NIST SP 800-22 R1a** A Statistical Test Suite for Random and Pseudorandom Number Generators for Cryptographic Applications
**NIST SP 800-30** Guide for Conducting Risk Assessments
**NIST SP 800-31** Intrusion Detection Systems
**NIST SP 800-32** Public Key Technology and the Federal PKI Infrastructure
**NIST SP 800-34 R1** Contingency Planning Guide for Federal Information Systems
**NIST SP 800-35** Guide to Information Technology Security Services
**NIST SP 800-36** Guide to Selecting Information Technology Security Products
**NIST SP 800-37 R2** Applying Risk Management Framework to Federal Information
**NIST SP 800-38** Recommendation for Block Cipher Modes of Operation
**NIST SP 800-38A Addendum** Block Cipher Modes of Operation: Three Variants of Ciphertext Stealing for CBC Mode
**NIST SP 800-38B** Block Cipher Modes of Operation: The CMAC Mode for Authentication
**NIST SP 800-38C** Block Cipher Modes of Operation: The CCM Mode for Authentication and Confidentiality
**NIST SP 800-38D** Block Cipher Modes of Operation: Galois/Counter Mode (GCM) and GMAC
**NIST SP 800-38E** Block Cipher Modes of Operation: The XTS-AES Mode for Confidentiality on Storage Devices
**NIST SP 800-38F** Block Cipher Modes of Operation: Methods for Key Wrapping
**NIST SP 800-38G** Block Cipher Modes of Operation: Methods for Format-Preserving Encryption
**NIST SP 800-39** Managing Information Security Risk
**NIST SP 800-40 R3** Guide to Enterprise Patch Management Technologies
**NIST SP 800-41** Guidelines on Firewalls and Firewall Policy
**NIST SP 800-44 V2** Guidelines on Securing Public Web Servers
**NIST SP 800-45 V2** Guidelines on Electronic Mail Security
**NIST SP 800-46 R2** Guide to Enterprise Telework, Remote Access, and Bring Your Own Device (BYOD) Security
**NIST SP 800-47** Security Guide for Interconnecting Information Technology Systems
**NIST SP 800-48** Guide to Securing Legacy IEEE 802.11 Wireless Networks
**NIST SP 800-49** Federal S/MIME V3 Client Profile
**NIST SP 800-50** Building an Information Technology Security Awareness and Training Program
**NIST SP 800-52 R1** Guidelines for the Selection, Configuration, and Use of Transport Layer Security (TLS) Implementations
**NIST SP 800-53 R5** Security and Privacy Controls for Information Systems and Organizations
**NIST SP 800-53A R4** Assessing Security and Privacy Controls
**NIST SP 800-54** Border Gateway Protocol Security
**NIST SP 800-56A R3** Pair-Wise Key-Establishment Schemes Using Discrete Logarithm Cryptography
**NIST SP 56B R 1** Recommendation for Pair-Wise Key-Establishment Schemes Using Integer Factorization Cryptography
**NIST SP 800-56C R1** Recommendation for Key-Derivation Methods in Key-Establishment Schemes - Draft
**NIST SP 800-57 R4** Recommendation for Key Management
**NIST SP 800-58** Security Considerations for Voice Over IP Systems
**NIST SP 800-60** Guide for Mapping Types of Information and Information Systems to Security Categories
**NIST SP 800-61 R2** Computer Security Incident Handling Guide
**NIST SP 800-63-3** Digital Identity Guidelines
**NIST SP 800-63a** Digital Identity Guidelines - Enrollment and Identity Proofing
**NIST SP 800-63b** Digital Identity Guidelines - Authentication and Lifecycle Management
**NIST SP 800-63c** Digital Identity Guidelines- Federation and Assertions
**NIST SP 800-64 R2** Security Considerations in the System Development Life Cycle
**NIST SP 800-66** Implementing the Health Insurance Portability and Accountability Act (HIPAA) Security Rule
**NIST SP 800-67 R2** Recommendation for Triple Data Encryption Algorithm (TDEA) Block Cipher - Draft
**NIST SP 800-70 R4** National Checklist Program for IT Products
**NIST SP 800-72** Guidelines on PDA Forensics
**NIST SP 800-73-4** Interfaces for Personal Identity Verification
**NIST SP 800-76-2** Biometric Specifications for Personal Identity Verification
**NIST SP 800-77** Guide to IPsec VPNs
**NIST SP 800-79-2** Authorization of Personal Identity Verification Card Issuers (PCI) and Derived PIV Credential Issuers (DPCI)
**NIST SP 800-81-2** Secure Domain Name System (DNS) Deployment Guide
**NIST SP 800-82 R2** Guide to Industrial Control Systems (ICS) Security
**NIST SP 800-83** Guide to Malware Incident Prevention and Handling for Desktops and Laptops
**NIST SP 800-84** Guide to Test, Training, and Exercise Programs for IT Plans and Capabilities
**NIST SP 800-85A-4 PIV** Card Application and Middleware Interface Test Guidelines
**NIST SP 800-85B-4 PIV** Data Model Test Guidelines - Draft
**NIST SP 800-86** Guide to Integrating Forensic Techniques into Incident Response

**NIST SP 800-88 R1** Guidelines for Media Sanitization

**NIST SP 800-90A R1** Random Number Generation Using Deterministic Random Bit Generators

**NIST SP 800-90B** Recommendation for the Entropy Sources Used for Random Bit Generation

**NIST SP 800-90C** Recommendation for Random Bit Generator (RBG) Constructions - 2nd Draft

**NIST SP 800-92** Guide to Computer Security Log Management

**NIST SP 800-94** Guide to Intrusion Detection and Prevention Systems (IDPS)

**NIST SP 800-95** Guide to Secure Web Services

**NIST SP 800-97** Establishing Wireless Robust Security Networks: A Guide to IEEE 802.11i

**NIST SP 800-98** Guidelines for Securing Radio Frequency Identification (RFID) Systems

**NIST SP 800-101 R1** Guidelines on Mobile Device Forensics

**NIST SP 800-107 R1** Recommendation for Applications Using Approved Hash Algorithms

**NIST SP 800-111** Guide to Storage Encryption Technologies for End User Devices

**NIST SP 800-113** Guide to SSL VPNs

**NIST SP 800-114 R1** User's Guide to Telework and Bring Your Own Device (BYOD) Security

**NIST SP 800-115** Technical Guide to Information Security Testing and Assessment

**NIST SP 800-116** A Recommendation for the Use of PIV Credentials in PACS - Draft

**NIST SP 800-119** Guidelines for the Secure Deployment of IPv6

**NIST SP 800-120** Recommendation for EAP Methods Used in Wireless Network Access Authentication

**NIST SP 800-121 R2** Guide to Bluetooth Security

**NIST SP 800-122** Guide to Protecting the Confidentiality of Personally Identifiable Information

**NIST SP 800-123** Guide to General Server Security

**NIST SP 800-124 R1** Managing the Security of Mobile Devices in the Enterprise

**NIST SP 800-125 (A & B)** Secure Virtual Network Configuration for Virtual Machine (VM) Protection

**NIST SP 800-126 R3** Technical Specification for the Security Content Automation Protocol (SCAP)

**NIST SP 800-127** Guide to Securing WiMAX Wireless Communications

**NIST SP 800-128** Guide for Security-Focused Configuration Management of Information Systems

**NIST SP 800-130** A Framework for Designing Cryptographic Key Management Systems

**NIST SP 800-131A R1** Transitions: Recommendation for Transitioning the Use of Cryptographic Algorithms and Key Lengths

**NIST SP 800-133** Recommendation for Cryptographic Key Generation

**NIST SP 800-137** Information Security Continuous Monitoring (ISCM)

**NIST SP 800-142** Practical Combinatorial Testing

**NIST SP 800-144** Guidelines on Security and Privacy in Public Cloud Computing

**NIST SP 800-145** The NIST Definition of Cloud Computing

**NIST SP 800-146** Cloud Computing Synopsis and Recommendations

**NIST SP 800-147** BIOS Protection Guidelines & BIOS Integrity Measurement Guidelines

**NIST SP 800-147B** BIOS Protection Guidelines for Servers

**NIST SP 800-150** Guide to Cyber Threat Information Sharing

**NIST SP 800-152** A Profile for U.S. Federal Cryptographic Key Management Systems

**NIST SP 800-153** Guidelines for Securing Wireless Local Area Networks (WLANs)

**NIST SP 800-154** Guide to Data-Centric System Threat Modeling

**NIST SP 800-155** BIOS Integrity Measurement Guidelines

**NIST SP 800-156** Representation of PIV Chain-of-Trust for Import and Export

**NIST SP 800-157** Guidelines for Derived Personal Identity Verification (PIV) Credentials

**NIST SP 800-160** Systems Security Engineering

**NIST SP 800-161** Supply Chain Risk Management Practices for Federal Information Systems and Organizations

**NIST SP 800-162** Guide to Attribute Based Access Control (ABAC) Definition and Considerations

**NIST SP 800-163** Vetting the Security of Mobile Applications

**NIST SP 800-164** Guidelines on Hardware- Rooted Security in Mobile Devices Draft

**NIST SP 800-166** Derived PIV Application and Data Model Test Guidelines

**NIST SP 800-167** Guide to Application Whitelisting

**NIST SP 800-171 R1** Protecting Controlled Unclassified Information in Nonfederal Systems

**NIST SP 800-175 (A & B)** Guideline for Using Cryptographic Standards in the Federal Government

**NIST SP 800-177 R1** Trustworthy Email (DRAFT 2)

**NIST SP 800-178** Comparison of Attribute Based Access Control (ABAC) Standards for Data Service Applications

**NIST SP 800-179** Guide to Securing Apple OS X 10.10 Systems for IT Professional

**NIST SP 800-181** National Initiative for Cybersecurity Education (NICE) Cybersecurity Workforce Framework

**NIST SP 800-183** Networks of 'Things'

**NIST SP 800-184** Guide for Cybersecurity Event Recovery

**NIST SP 800-187** Guide to LTE Security - Draft

**NIST SP 800-188** De-Identifying Government Datasets - (2nd Draft)

**NIST SP 800-190** Application Container Security Guide

**NIST SP 800-191** The NIST Definition of Fog Computing

**NIST SP 800-192** Verification and Test Methods for Access Control Policies/Models

**NIST SP 800-193** Platform Firmware Resiliency Guidelines

**NIST SP 1800-1** Securing Electronic Health Records on Mobile Devices

**NIST SP 1800-2** Identity and Access Management for Electric Utilities 1800-2a & 1800-2b

**NIST SP 1800-2** Identity and Access Management for Electric Utilities 1800-2c

**NIST SP 1800-3** Attribute Based Access Control NIST 1800-3a & 3b

**NIST SP 1800-3** Attribute Based Access Control NIST 1800-3c Chapters 1 - 6

**NIST SP 1800-3** Attribute Based Access Control NIST1800-3c Chapters 7 - 10

**NIST SP 1800-4a & 4b** Mobile Device Security: Cloud and Hybrid Builds
**NIST SP 1800-4c** Mobile Device Security: Cloud and Hybrid Builds
**NIST SP 1800-5** IT Asset Management: Financial Services
**NIST SP 1800-6** Domain Name Systems-Based Electronic Mail Security
**NIST SP 1800-7** Situational Awareness for Electric Utilities
**NIST SP 1800-8** Securing Wireless Infusion Pumps
**NIST SP 1800-9a & 9b** Access Rights Management for the Financial Services Sector
**NIST SP 1800-9c** Access Rights Management for the Financial Services Sector - How To Guide
**NIST SP 1800-11a & 11b** Data Integrity Recovering from Ransomware and Other Destructive Events
**NIST SP 1800-11c** Data Integrity Recovering from Ransomware and Other Destructive Events - How To Guide
**NIST SP 1800-12** Derived Personal Identity Verification (PIV) Credentials
**NISTIR 7298 R2** Glossary of Key Information Security Terms
**NISTIR 7316** Assessment of Access Control Systems
**NISTIR 7497** Security Architecture Design Process for Health Information Exchanges (HIEs)
**NISTIR 7511 R4 V1.2** Security Content Automation Protocol (SCAP) Version 1.2 Validation Program Test Requirements
**NISTIR 7628 R1 Vol 1** Guidelines for Smart Grid Cybersecurity - Architecture, and High-Level Requirements
**NISTIR 7628 R1 Vol 2** Guidelines for Smart Grid Cybersecurity - Privacy and the Smart Grid
**NISTIR 7628 R1 Vol 3** Guidelines for Smart Grid Cybersecurity - Supportive Analyses and References
**NISTIR 7756** CAESARS Framework Extension: An Enterprise Continuous Monitoring Technical Refer
**NISTIR 7788** Security Risk Analysis of Enterprise Networks Using Probabilistic Attack Graphs
**NISTIR 7823** Advanced Metering Infrastructure Smart Meter Upgradeability Test Framework
**NISTIR 7874** Guidelines for Access Control System Evaluation Metrics
**NISTIR 7904** Trusted Geolocation in the Cloud: Proof of Concept Implementation
**NISTIR 7924** Reference Certificate Policy
**NISTIR 7987** Policy Machine: Features, Architecture, and Specification
**NISTIR 8006** NIST Cloud Computing Forensic Science Challenges
**NISTIR 8011 Vol 1** Automation Support for Security Control Assessments
**NISTIR 8011 Vol 2** Automation Support for Security Control Assessments
**NISTIR 8040** Measuring the Usability and Security of Permuted Passwords on Mobile Platforms
**NISTIR 8053** De-Identification of Personal Information
**NISTIR 8054** NSTIC Pilots: Catalyzing the Identity Ecosystem
**NISTIR 8055** Derived Personal Identity Verification (PIV) Credentials (DPC) Proof of Concept Research
**NISTIR 8060** Guidelines for the Creation of Interoperable Software Identification (SWID) Tags
**NISTIR 8062** Introduction to Privacy Engineering and Risk Management in Federal Systems
**NISTIR 8074 Vol 1 & Vol 2** Strategic U.S. Government Engagement in International Standardization to Achieve U.S. Objectives for Cybersecurity
**NISTIR 8080** Usability and Security Considerations for Public Safety Mobile Authentication
**NISTIR 8089** An Industrial Control System Cybersecurity Performance Testbed
**NISTIR 8112** Attribute Metadata - Draft
**NISTIR 8135** Identifying and Categorizing Data Types for Public Safety Mobile Applications
**NISTIR 8138** Vulnerability Description Ontology (VDO)
**NISTIR 8144** Assessing Threats to Mobile Devices & Infrastructure
**NISTIR 8151** Dramatically Reducing Software Vulnerabilities
**NISTIR 8170** The Cybersecurity Framework
**NISTIR 8176** Security Assurance Requirements for Linux Application Container Deployments
**NISTIR 8179** Criticality Analysis Process Model
**NISTIR 8183** Cybersecurity Framework Manufacturing Profile
**NISTIR 8192** Enhancing Resilience of the Internet and Communications Ecosystem
**Whitepaper** Cybersecurity Framework Manufacturing Profile
**Whitepaper** NIST Framework for Improving Critical Infrastructure Cybersecurity
**Whitepaper** Challenging Security Requirements for US Government Cloud Computing Adoption
**FIPS PUBS 140-2** Security Requirements for Cryptographic Modules
**FIPS PUBS 140-2 Annex A** Approved Security Functions
**FIPS PUBS 140-2 Annex B** Approved Protection Profiles
**FIPS PUBS 140-2 Annex C** Approved Random Number Generators
**FIPS PUBS 140-2 Annex D** Approved Key Establishment Techniques
**FIPS PUBS 180-4** Secure Hash Standard (SHS)
**FIPS PUBS 186-4** Digital Signature Standard (DSS)
**FIPS PUBS 197** Advanced Encryption Standard (AES)
**FIPS PUBS 198-1** The Keyed-Hash Message Authentication Code (HMAC)
**FIPS PUBS 199** Standards for Security Categorization of Federal Information and Information Systems
**FIPS PUBS 200** Minimum Security Requirements for Federal Information and Information Systems
**FIPS PUBS 201-2** Personal Identity Verification (PIV) of Federal Employees and Contractors
**FIPS PUBS 202** SHA-3 Standard: Permutation-Based Hash and Extendable-Output Functions

**DHS Study** DHS Study on Mobile Device Security

**OMB A-130 / FISMA** OMB A-130/Federal Information Security Modernization Act
**GAO** Federal Information System Controls Audit Manual

| DoD | |
|---|---|
| UFC 3-430-11 | Boiler Control Systems |
| UFC 4-010-06 | Cybersecurity of Facility-Related Control Systems |
| FC 4-141-05N | Navy and Marine Corps Industrial Control Systems Monitoring Stations |
| MIL-HDBK-232A | RED/BLACK Engineering-Installation Guidelines |
| MIL-HDBK 1195 | Radio Frequency Shielded Enclosures |
| TM 5-601 | Supervisory Control and Data Acquisition (SCADA) Systems for C4ISR Facilities |
| ESTCP | Facility-Related Control Systems Cybersecurity Guideline |
| ESTCP | Facility-Related Control Systems Ver 4.0 |
| DoD | Self-Assessing Security Vulnerabilities & Risks of Industrial Controls |
| DoD | Program Manager's Guidebook for Integrating the Cybersecurity Risk Management Framework (RMF) into the System Acquisition Lifecycle |
| DoD | Advanced Cyber Industrial Control System Tactics, Techniques, and Procedures (ACI TTP) |
| DoD 4140.1 | Supply Chain Materiel Management Procedures |
| AFI 17-2NAS | Network Attack System (NAS) Vol. 1, 2 & 3 |
| AFI 17-2ACD | Air Force Cyberspace Defense (ACD) Vol. 1, 2 & 3 |
| AFI 10-1703 | Air Force Cyberspace Training Publications |
| AFPD 17-2 | Air Force Cyberspace Operations |
| AFI 17-2CSCS | Air Force Cyberspace Security and Control System (CSCS) Vol. 1, 2 & 3 |

www.ingramcontent.com/pod-product-compliance
Lightning Source LLC
LaVergne TN
LVHW060143070326
832902LV00018B/2921